A Vine-Ripened Life

A Vine-Ripened Life

Spiritual Fruitfulness through
Abiding in Christ

Stanley D. Gale

Reformation Heritage Books
Grand Rapids, Michigan

A Vine-Ripened Life
© 2014 by Stanley D. Gale

Reformation Heritage Books
2965 Leonard St. NE
Grand Rapids, MI 49525
616-977-0889 / Fax 616-285-3246
orders@heritagebooks.org
www.heritagebooks.org

Printed in the United States of America
14 15 16 17 18 19/10 9 8 7 6 5 4 3 2 1

Library of Congress Cataloging-in-Publication Data

Gale, Stanley D., 1953-
   A vine-ripened life : spiritual fruitfulness through abiding in Christ / Stanley D. Gale.
      pages cm
   ISBN 978-1-60178-343-1 (pbk. : alk. paper) 1. Fruit of the Spirit. 2. Christian life. I. Title.
   BV4501.3.G355 2014
   248.4—dc23
                                        2014015204

For additional Reformed literature, request a free book list from Reformation Heritage Books at the above regular or e-mail address.

This book is dedicated to the latest additions
to my quiver of grandchildren:

Gryphon and Penelope

But the mercy of the LORD is from everlasting to everlasting
On those who fear Him,
And His righteousness to children's children,
To such as keep His covenant,
And to those who remember His commandments to do them.

—PSALM 103:17–18

Contents

Preface

Choosing a title for a book is always tricky business. While it's true that judging a book by its cover is frowned upon as imprudent, a cover presents that split-second first impression that prompts a reader to peer within. While the cover appeals to the eye, the title spread across it speaks more to the ear. It grabs our attention—or it doesn't. As part of that initial impression, the potential reader decides if a book is worth his or her time.

I'm well pleased with the title of the volume you hold. You've made it this far likely because it spoke something that intrigued you, prompting you to pick it up. But the idea for the book did not set sail under the title *A Vine-Ripened Life*. Rather, the prospective title was *A Grace-Grown Life*. That title was demoted and abbreviated for the final chapter.

A Grace-Grown Life does sound catchy—and relevant. As you'll see when you arrive at the final chapter, grace plays an integral role in Christian growth and fruitfulness. The grace that inaugurates the Christian life is the grace that stimulates fruit and maturity. But I rejected that initial title as inadequate. The grace in view, the grace that impacts our lives, comes to us through a person—Jesus Christ. It is by abiding in Him that we bear much fruit, fruit that will endure. He is the Vine; we are the branches. Apart from Christ we can do nothing. Through Christ who strengthens us, we can do all things.

To speak of a "vine-ripened" life points us to Jesus. Jesus describes Himself as the Vine of life (see John 15) through whom we live and grow and bear the fruit of a grace-grown life. We ripen on the Vine, where we grow to bear the expected fruit of new life. Having begun in Christ we remain in Christ, continuing to draw our life from Him and maturing in grace.

"Vine-ripened" holds the prospect of not learning merely *about* the fruit of Christian character but learning *how* to cultivate that fruit. We bear fruit through abiding in Christ. But what does that mean? How do we go about it? That's all part of the package we examine as we undertake the study before us.

Basically, this book explores the fruit of the Spirit. The classic passage of the Bible that explicitly inventories the fruit is found in Paul's letter to the Galatians: "But the fruit of the Spirit is love, joy, peace, longsuffering, kindness, goodness, faithfulness, gentleness, self-control. Against such there is no law" (5:22–23). This list is the most extensive, but it is not exclusive. For example, we find an abridged version in Paul's charge to Timothy: "Pursue righteousness, godliness, faith, love, patience, gentleness" (1 Tim. 6:11).

For the most part, however, we will limit our study to the nine traits of Galatians 5, opting to include humility as a bonus feature for reasons that will become apparent. Each and every fruit in the bounty of the Spirit, though, germinates in us through union with Christ as the Vine of life and grows lush through abiding in Christ. It is that note which escorts us to the first stop of our study in chapter 1, "Fruit of the Vine."

This book is undergirded with encouragers and influencers. I am deeply grateful to them and to God for raising them up in my life. My wife, Linda, comprises the vanguard of that group. I can always count on her for honest observation, tempered with loving support. Alexandra, Gretchen, Audra, and Stephen are, along with me, part of a writers' group. Their insights have made this book more cohesive and readable. I have greatly benefited from the practical prodding of a friend and fellow author, Leslie Montgomery. She gave me moral support, reassurance in the project, and help in guiding it to publication. I am indebted to John Sanderson and Jerry Bridges, who have also written on the subject. They have both stimulated my thinking and enriched my understanding. I want to acknowledge Dwight Dunn, a fellow pastor and time-tested friend. This book is owed in large part to his faithfulness in prayer for me. I would be remiss were I to neglect offering special thanks to Jay Collier and Reformation Heritage Books for their willingness to bring the book to fruition and their encouragement in its value, and to Annette Gysen, with whom it was a pleasure to work in the editing process.

—SDG

Chapter 1

Fruit of the Vine

I am the vine, you are the branches.
He who abides in Me, and I in him, bears much fruit;
for without Me you can do nothing.
—JOHN 15:5

My wife and I are officially empty nesters. After thirty-three years of having at least one child at home, we are now left with just our dog. We recently deposited our last born, Nathan, in western Pennsylvania to begin his studies at Grove City College. It seems it wasn't that long ago that Nathan emerged from the womb to enter our home. Now he's leaving to enter college. I remember watching him jump his highest in an effort to touch the top of the doorway to our living room. Now his head almost brushes against it.

Nathan has entered the next phase of his life. That's a good thing (I keep reminding myself). He has grown in every way: physically, spiritually, intellectually, and relationally. His mother and I take some credit for that growth. We fed and clothed him, supervised his studies, and cultivated friendships.

We also raised him in the nurture and admonition of the Lord, living out the gospel before him through our instruction and example. Nathan also had a role, though. He ate the food we provided. As he grew into a teenager, he ate more than we provided. His going to college halved our food bill.

But what caused Nathan to grow? What spurred on his physical development into the strapping young man that he is? I would suggest that it was not just the food. It was the way his body worked to assimilate that food to his physical growth and nourishment. God designed his body to act upon that intake.

That's how sanctification works. We, as believers, take in the nourishment of God's Word. That Word enters the open mouth of our minds. We chew on it through study and meditation. Prayer aids in its digestion to our spiritual nourishment and growth in grace.

The Westminster Shorter Catechism defines *sanctification*: "Sanctification is the work of God's grace, wherein we are renewed in the whole man, after the image of God; and are enabled to die more and more unto sin; and live more and more unto righteousness" (Q&A 35). This definition offers a comprehensive explanation. It describes the breadth of the sanctifying process (the whole man); the goal (the renewed image of God); and the process itself (die to sin and live to righteousness).

Another way we can look at the spiritual growth process of sanctification is by way of fruit. In His Upper Room Discourse in John 13 to 17, Jesus talks about fruit: "Abide in Me, and I in you. As the branch cannot bear fruit of itself, unless it abides in the vine, neither can you, unless you abide in Me.

I am the vine, you are the branches. He who abides in Me, and I in him, bears much fruit; for without Me you can do nothing" (15:4–5). Among the fruit to which Jesus refers is that of a changed life, which flows out of being partakers of the new life bound up in Christ. Abiding in Christ produces "much fruit," fruit that will last (15:5, 16).

In this metaphor Jesus indicates that abiding is accomplished in large part through utter dependence on Him. The grace of sanctification flows from experiential union with Christ. We must abide in Christ so that the fruit of character change in our lives is not the product of self-will or best effort. Such efforts at love or joy or patience will be meager and short lived.

We want the fruit of a changed life to grow organically and not artificially. Organic spiritual fruit grows from the good soil of a well-tended heart. Artificial fruit is akin to religious hypocrisy that is different in public than it is in private. Such fruit is as removable as an article of clothing, detachable as false eyelashes.

But artificial fruit is not merely the product of pretense. It can flow from good intentions as well. We try our best to be patient, loving, or self-controlled. We know that's what our Father wants of us. We want it for ourselves. But our best efforts will produce only imitation fruit. It may look great in our eyes and others', but it is not the fruit of abiding in the Vine. We want the fruit of a changed life to grow from the inside out by the hand of our God—a Vine-ripened life. Let's enter this vineyard of life and explore God's design for our spiritual development and growth in grace.

Fruit of the Vine

Complete the following: Red, white, and _____. Most people, especially if they are Americans, would reflexively write *blue* in the blank. Let's try another: Peanut butter and _____. There are those who might fill in *banana* or *marshmallow*, but I suspect 90 percent of respondents would write *jelly*. One more: Fruit of the _____. My guess is those reading this book would automatically respond *Spirit* (if they had not been tipped off by the chapter title).

Normally when we think of fruit related to Christian character, we think of fruit of the Spirit. Fruit of the Vine, on the other hand, brings to mind Jesus' words at the institution of the Lord's Supper, not character qualities. But actually, fruit of the Vine gives us a better orientation to what our heavenly Father has in mind for us.

How do we grow as Christians? Does the Holy Spirit just come to us on His own, like one of those independent contractors who knocks on our door asking if we want a free estimate on home repair? Does He just show up to start a spiritual makeover of us? No, He brings Christ to us and us to Christ.

Jesus made it clear in John 15 that fruitfulness in the Christian life comes from abiding in Him as the Vine. Both before and after His teaching on fruitfulness in John 15, Jesus speaks of the Holy Spirit in John 14 and 16. The production of "much fruit" in John 15:5 is framed by the work of the Holy Spirit whom Jesus would send upon His ascension. Like a power cord to a wall outlet, the Holy Spirit conveys the life, power, and fruitfulness of Christ to us for our growth in grace.

Rather than calling the fruit of the Christian life "the fruit of the Spirit," we might call it the "fruit of abiding in

Christ through the Holy Spirit who unites us to Him." "Fruit of the Spirit" is shorthand for God's handiwork of grace to conform us to Christ. The fruit the Spirit works in us is not apart from Christ, but is bound up in Christ. We abound in that fruit through abiding in Christ. The fruit of new life comes about through union with Christ that flows from the inside out. It grows from the good soil of a changed heart that is transformed by God's Spirit.

I was laid up following surgery. Turning the tables on pastoral visitation, a woman from my church and a friend visited me at my home. They thoughtfully brought me one of those edible arrangements, fresh fruit cut to look like flowers. It had pineapple blossoms, cantaloupe and honeydew leaves, strawberry buds, and grape sprigs. It was pleasing to the eye and to the taste.

As beautiful as that fruit was, it would not last. It would not multiply. No matter how well tended, it would spoil. But the fruit God wants of us will grow heartily by virtue of being united to Jesus Christ as the Vine of life. It will display the grace and vigor of God's workmanship as the Vinedresser. It will be Christlike, Christ drawn—like a flower draws life-giving nutrients from the soil in which it is rooted.

This fruit will not be produced by sheer willpower or determination to be more loving or patient or kind. Those of us who have attempted to produce fruit by our own efforts have learned how fruitless that is. Rather, bountiful and enduring Christlike character will grow organically by abiding in Christ, through the operation of the Holy Spirit.

As we explore the fruit of the Spirit, our approach will not be self-reformation: no "get your act together" or kick-in-the-pants "try harder." If we come away from this study without a deeper knowledge of Christ and more profound dependence upon Him, we have missed the point.

The Fruit of the Spirit Is...

A crisis in the English language exists today. People don't know how to use proper grammar any longer. On top of that, it seems that errors are so commonplace that they are being accepted as proper. For example, it is common to hear, "He gave some fruit to Betty and I." But *I* is a subject pronoun. It doesn't belong as an object of the preposition *to*. Proper grammar would dictate "He gave some fruit to Betty and me."

What are we to think, then, when we turn to Galatians 5 and find Paul saying in verse 22 that "the *fruit* of the Spirit *is* love, joy, peace," and so forth. Wouldn't subject-verb agreement dictate "fruits...are" since multiple fruits are mentioned?

No, when a writer uses grammar in a way that seems improper, we should examine his or her reason rather than assume a mistake. What is Paul telling us? Some say that the verb is singular because Paul is just speaking singularly about love. All the other fruits flow from love, just like we see patience (or longsuffering) and kindness in the description of love in 1 Corinthians 13. Love is a blossom layered in the petals of joy, peace, patience, and the rest, fragrant with the scent of grace.

That image is certainly lovely and poetic. But there is another possible reason for Paul's sentence structure. In the New Testament, we are taught of the *gifts* of the Spirit and the *fruit* of the Spirit. When Paul speaks of the gifts of the Spirit, he refers to many gifts: some in speaking, some in serving, and some in giving. Not every believer has every gift. For example, I believe my gift involves teaching. I don't have the gift of singing, or any musical ability for that matter. At the counsel of others, I turn my microphone off before I join in singing a hymn from the pulpit.

However, when it comes to the fruit of the Spirit, *all* believers are to manifest *every* fruit of Christlikeness, every character quality of godliness that belongs to new life in Christ. We don't have the option of picking six of nine or even eight of nine from the list in Galatians 5:22–23. We can't say, "Oh, I'm just not a patient person" and so excuse ourselves from that fruit in our lives. We have no ground to rationalize our lack of self-control by saying, "I'm only human." Just as there is one Christ, so the fruit of the Spirit that flows from our union with Him is expressive of one character. In fact, the list in Galatians 5 is itself not exhaustive in describing Christian character. The Bible talks about other fruit, like righteousness and humility, both exhibited in Christ and in which we are to grow.

Moreover, we can never fall into the trap of believing our natural strengths and abilities substitute for the redemptive characteristics of life in Christ. We can't think, "Hey, I'm already gentle," or, "I have self-control. I don't need to abide in Christ for those." We need to find our capability in *both* our weaknesses and our strengths through abiding in Christ.

Fruit Formation

A pastor friend wrote an article on the subject of discipleship. He stressed that a threefold response to the call of Christ is required: repentance, faith, and following. None of these contribute to our salvation, but all of them are the fruit of God's work of grace in our lives. Discipleship involves more than development of Christian character, but it does involve such character as a matter of first importance. In the Bible, a disciple is not just a student, but one who becomes like his teacher.

We are to grow in the character of Christ our Lord. While that growth is by grace at the hand of God, we are actively involved in the cultivation of the fruit of a godly life. We'll see this in practical terms as we explore various fruit of the Vine in the chapters ahead. But we can note this now: every fruit of a Christlike life is presented to us as both a noun and a verb. For each of the nouns listed in Galatians 5:22–23, we can find corresponding verbs and commands elsewhere: to love, to rejoice, to exercise peace, to be patient, and to be kind and forgiving.

Yet this fruit is formed by reliance on the Holy Spirit. Paul brackets the fruit of the Spirit in Galatians 5 with this emphasis and strategy: "I say then: Walk in the Spirit, and you shall not fulfill the lust of the flesh" (Gal. 5:16). "If we live in the Spirit, let us also walk in the Spirit" (Gal. 5:25). Though we are called to purpose and to do, we are completely dependent on the Spirit to act and to achieve anything genuine and lasting.

Notice also that we are not simply to stop indulging in sexual impurity or deal with our anger issues by biting our tongues. Galatians 5:16 instructs us that as we "walk in the Spirit," we "shall not fulfill the lust of the flesh." Like some oak trees produce new leaves by pushing out the old ones, so we grow out of the old character we had before our conversion by pursuing the new character in Christ.

This is no trivial endeavor. At its heart is a battle. When we diet, we fight the battle of the waistline. Our cravings for food wage war with our desire for a smaller us. Spiritual growth involves spiritual warfare, confronting the desires of the flesh and refusing to be ruled by them (Gal. 5:17). We cannot live as though we are still in bondage to the kingdom of Satan (Gal. 5:21). We have been emancipated from servitude to sin and empowered for the new life.

Freedom from bondage to sin for development of the fruit of the Spirit is forged by union with Christ (Gal. 5:24). Growth in the spiritual formation of the fruit of the Spirit will involve learning to abide in Christ. The question is, How do we go about abiding?

Abide to Abound

Abiding is Christ's strategy for spiritual fruitfulness. We can capture the essence of abiding through three phrases we find in Scripture.

"Jesus Christ, whom having not seen you love" (1 Peter 1:7–8). Abiding begins and continues with a focus on the person and work of Jesus Christ, in whom we have life and through whom we experience growth (cf. Gal. 2:20). In view is not just the person of Christ, but the personal Christ. The heart of an abiding Christian life is a love relationship with Him who loved us and gave His life for us. Peter sets the tone: "Jesus Christ, whom having not seen you love. Though now you do not see Him, yet believing, you rejoice with joy inexpressible and full of glory" (1 Peter 1:7–8).

Abiding lives out our newfound fellowship with the Father and the Son. When Jesus says in John 15:5 that we are to abide in Him, He characterizes the nature of that abiding. It is not mechanical, but relational. Jesus says: "As the Father loved Me, I also have loved you; abide in My love" (John 15:9).

"Let the word of Christ dwell in you richly" (Col. 3:16). In Colossians 3, Paul informs us that our "life is hidden with Christ in God" and that Christ is our life (vv. 3–4). From that point of reference, we are to "put off" the old man and "put on" the new, including character traits like "kindness, humility, meekness" (vv. 9, 12). In this context Paul directs us to let the word of Christ dwell in us richly.

Colossians and Ephesians are sister epistles, paralleling each other in content and order of presentation. In parallel to letting the word of Christ dwell in them richly, as he puts it to the Colossians, Paul writes to the Ephesians that they should not get drunk with wine but "be filled with the Spirit" (5:18). These statements in sister epistles are epexegetical, helping to explain one another, tying together Word and Spirit.

We abide in Christ by letting His Word dwell in us richly—not just those words in red letters in some of our Bibles, but the whole Word of God. Jesus highlights this as a means for abiding when He says, "You abide in Me, and My words abide in you" (John 15:7). In Jesus' High Priestly Prayer that comes late in the Upper Room Discourse, He ties the word into our sanctification: "Sanctify them by Your truth. Your word is truth" (John 17:17).

"Praying always with all prayer and supplication in the Spirit" (Eph. 6:18). Prayer is indispensable to abiding. Through it we express complete and continual dependence on Christ, as well as communion with Him. Jesus ties our spiritual fruitfulness into our prayers: "You did not choose Me, but I chose you and appointed you that you should go and bear fruit, and that your fruit should remain, that whatever you ask the Father in My name He may give you" (John 15:16). Abiding fruit comes by way of abiding prayer.

As competent as the apostle Paul was, he saw the need for prayer for any enduring fruit in his ministry. In light of the goal of fruitfulness and in light of our enemy the devil, who opposes fruitfulness, Paul urges us on, "praying always with all prayer and supplication in the Spirit, being watchful to this end with all perseverance and supplication for all the saints" (Eph. 6:18).

We need to consider one last thing about abiding. Certainly, abiding is an individual matter, something to which we must each give attention. Yet each of these aforementioned aspects of abiding is cultivated in community as well. We pray with and for one another. We teach and admonish one another in application of the Word. We love one another and stimulate a love for Christ. Christ's church is a greenhouse for growth.

Conclusion

In Numbers 13, after the people of Israel had been brought out of slavery in Egypt but before they had settled in the Promised Land, a group of twelve men was assembled to do some reconnaissance in their future home. What were the people like there? What were the cities like? Moses instructed them to bring back this intelligence as well as some fruit of the land.

When the twelve returned, they carried a single cluster of grapes they had cut down from the Valley of Eschol. That single cluster was so bountiful and so burgeoning with fruit it took two men to carry it on a pole between them.

That is a picture of what God has for us in the Promised Land of our life in Christ. God's design for us is not withered, meager fruit. He doesn't want wax fruit we have fashioned ourselves as decoration for our lives. Jesus says that if we abide in Him we will bear *much* fruit—the fruit of an authentically changed life, the fruit of impact and influence for Christ. Jesus also says this: "By this My Father is glorified, that you bear much fruit; so you will be My disciples" (John 15:8).

So the question is, Is the fruit of God's grace, the fruit that flows from saving faith, growing in your life? Is it defining you? Do others see it and so give glory to your Father in heaven? As we embark on our study, let us pray even now for God's workmanship of grace in our lives and the lives of our brothers and sisters in Christ—to the glory of His name.

Cultivating Growth

1. What is sanctification?

2. How does sanctification parallel physical maturation?

3. What is our involvement in our sanctification? What is God's? How is this mutual involvement seen in Philippians 2:12–13?

4. How does the metaphor of abiding in the Vine from John 15 help us in pursuing spiritual growth?

5. What does it mean for the fruit of the Spirit to grow organically? With what is organic contrasted?

6. What is the difference between the gifts of the Spirit and the fruit of the Spirit?

7. In practical terms, how do we go about abiding in Christ?

Chapter 2

My Father, the Gardener

I am the true vine, and My Father is the vinedresser.
Every branch in Me that does not bear fruit He takes away;
and every branch that bears fruit He prunes,
that it may bear more fruit.

—JOHN 15:1–2

Jesus tells us our Father is the Vinedresser. He is the gardener who tends us for the production of fruit in our lives. He is at work cultivating us to produce *more* fruit, toward His goal for us of *much* fruit, fruit that will endure. As our Father, God has a vested interest in our spiritual development. We are the workmanship of His grace. One of God's stated purposes for His redemption of us is the fruit of a changed life, toward demonstrating Christlike character (Eph. 2:10; Titus 2:11–14).

Just as an earthly father is concerned for the socialization of his children, so our heavenly Father is concerned for the sanctification of His children. Our God is a hands-on Father, interested and involved in our lives to conform us to the image of His begotten Son.

Need for Attention

What happens when we let our gardens at home go untended? They become a mess. Weeds spring up everywhere, choking what we have planted. The vegetables or flowers either do not grow or are stunted in their growth because of the presence of weeds, which steal nutrients from the good plants and bully their way to prominence. The result is not a pretty sight!

That's the way it works with us as well. The sin that remains in us produces weeds. Paul describes these as the "works of the flesh":

> Now the works of the flesh are evident, which are: adultery, fornication, uncleanness, lewdness, idolatry, sorcery, hatred, contentions, jealousies, outbursts of wrath, selfish ambitions, dissensions, heresies, envy, murders, drunkenness, revelries, and the like; of which I tell you beforehand, just as I also told you in time past, that those who practice such things will not inherit the kingdom of God. (Gal. 5:19–21)

Like the weeds we wrestle with in our gardens, these weeds of the flesh grow up with surprising vigor and little help from us. The more we allow them to grow, the more robust and deeply rooted they become.

I remember a tender stalk with fern-like leaves growing on the side of a hill in my yard. I knew it was a weed and didn't belong there. All I needed to do was pluck it up. I decided I'd get to it later, but later became months. The tender stalk became a tree trunk, turning from green to brown. When I realized what had happened, I decided it was time to act. I tried to pull it from the ground, but it was not budging. The root had become so deep and the plant so strong that I had to use loppers to cut it down. The plant was gone, but the root remained, producing shoots and continuing its efforts to propagate its unwanted and unsightly growth.

That's how sin left unchecked works in our lives. It needs immediate and constant attention. Our hearts are sin factories, generating product around the clock.

As our Father, God knows our hearts. He instructs earthly parents that sin is bound up in the heart of a child, which is why children need the wise, loving attention of a parent to tend and train them. Because children's hearts are sinful, Christian parents know well the importance of hands-on involvement in raising their children. Proverbs 22:6 instructs us: "Train up a child in the way he should go, and when he is old he will not depart from it." In one sense, that proverb holds out a wonderful promise, but at its core it presents a grave warning. Like the plant in my yard that I ignored, unchecked sin in a child's life can become more difficult to uproot.

The Scriptures apprise us that we are born into this world in sin. We are like cars out of alignment that, without firm hands on the steering wheel, will veer off the road. God's calling to parents to train their children in the way they should go is more a warning than a promise. The verse might better reflect the original language if it were translated like this: "Train up a child in the manner of his own eyes." That means if we adopt a laissez-faire approach to child rearing, we are doing a disservice to our children by not directing and protecting them.

Allowing a fallen image bearer to do what is right in "his own eyes" does nothing but cultivate rebellion against God. It constitutes Christian parental malpractice. Proverbs 14:12

observes, "There is a way that seems right to a man, but its end is the way of death." Do we want to allow our children to follow what seems right to them, knowing it will lead them from God and pit them against His truth and His way of life?

Another proverb states: "Chasten your son while there is hope, and do not set your heart on his destruction" (19:18). The world supposes that corporal punishment is child abuse. But God says, "He who spares his rod hates his son, but he who loves him disciplines him promptly" (Prov. 13:24). In God's wisdom, neglect of corporal punishment or unpleasant consequences to deter unwanted behavior is tantamount to child abuse, described as hating the child.

As God instructs earthly fathers in rearing their children, so He rears us. He tends us to weed out sin and cultivate fruit in our lives as our Father, the gardener. We understand that pruning is the discipline of our Father for our good.

What loving father hasn't at some point told his kids as he punished them, "I'm doing this because I love you"? Though his children may not believe him at the time, a dad who punishes his children is not being unloving. He is loving them by involving himself in their lives as he thinks best. He asserts his love because he wants his children to be assured that he has their best interest at heart, contrary to what they perceive as unloving and experience as unpleasant. The proverb urges us on to understand God's discipline in the same way:

> My son, do not despise the chastening of the LORD,
> Nor detest His correction;
> For whom the LORD loves He corrects,
> Just as a father the son in whom he delights.
>   (Prov. 3:11–12)

This theme is picked up in the New Testament book of Hebrews, where we are instructed about the cultivating work of our Father for the production of spiritual fruit in our lives as we mature in Christlike character.

Dare to Be Disciplined

Hebrews 12 begins by calling us to run the race of faith in a difficult and inhospitable world. The writer speaks of "weight" and "sin" that encumber us for that race (vv. 1–2). Later in the chapter he addresses challenges we face in our journey: "Therefore strengthen the hands which hang down, and the feeble knees, and make straight paths for your feet, so that what is lame may not be dislocated, but rather be healed" (vv. 12–13). We face challenges within and circumstances without in the race set before us.

Sandwiched in between, the writer quotes Proverbs 3:11–12 and then says this in verses 7–11:

> If you endure chastening, God deals with you as with sons; for what son is there whom a father does not chasten? But if you are without chastening, of which all have become partakers, then you are illegitimate and not sons. Furthermore, we have had human fathers who corrected us, and we paid them respect. Shall we not much more readily be in subjection to the Father of spirits and live? For they indeed for a few days chastened us as seemed best to them, but He for our profit, that we may be partakers of His holiness. Now no chastening seems to be joyful for the present, but painful; nevertheless, afterward it yields the peaceable fruit of righteousness to those who have been trained by it.

The writer of Hebrews couches the persecution of his readers within the will of God and governed by His fatherly hand, carrying His sanctifying purpose for them. He is saying their hardship is God's discipline, or chastening, to train them as His children and to equip them for the race of the Christian life.

Just as an earthly father would want his children to understand and to listen to him for their benefit, so our heavenly Father says that for His discipline to be beneficial, we must embrace it. We are not to "despise the chastening of the LORD." We are not to make light of God's work in our lives to discipline us. Knowing that pruning produces fruit, we want to endure it, confident of our Father's work and wisdom, and we want to embrace it, expecting a harvest of the fruit of righteousness in our lives.

Do Not Make Light

God gives His instruction negatively in Proverbs 3 and Hebrews 12 ("do not despise the chastening of the LORD") because He knows the resistance resident in our hearts. We see it mirrored in our children. So He tells us not to make light. The word translated *despise* means "to look down on; to have contempt for; to give no heed to." Any parent who has had teenagers can put a face to this admonition. God gives us three ways by which we can make light of His discipline in our lives.

Not Recognizing It

We make light of God's discipline by not recognizing it. A mom negotiates her shopping cart at the end of the checkout line in the grocery store. Her three-year-old sits unsteadily in the rumble seat, having been chauffeured through the aisles. As she relocates her supplies from the cart to the cashier's conveyor belt, her passenger falls prey to the nefarious plot of store managers to create family conflict by displaying candy at the eye level and arm's reach of most toddlers. "I want a candy bar," demands the child. "No," her mom says. The little girl reasserts her demand, this time competing with the public address system. On it goes, until the mom and daughter exit the store, groceries in hand, thirty pairs of eyes helping them out the door.

This is but one example of hundreds where parents intervene in their children's lives to do what is best to protect and train them. The three-year-old might not interpret her mother's refusal as anything but meanness, but any other parent will discern the boundaries drawn by the mom for the child's own good.

How well do we recognize those times in our lives when our heavenly Father deprives us of something we want or leads us into trials—both for our own good? James, a book on wisdom like Proverbs, says that we are to "count it all joy" when we encounter trials of various kinds. He even tells us why we are to do something so counterintuitive. The text goes on: "knowing that the testing of your faith produces patience" (1:2–3). The trial is for our training. It is like a piece of fitness equipment perfectly calibrated to meet us in our weakness and grow us in our faith as we exercise it.

The writer of Hebrews reminds us that God as our Father is at work in our lives to mold us into the image of Christ as son and servant. We are to "endure" discipline (12:7). The word *endure* does not mean just "to put up with," like a sister would her brother's teasing. It means to "hold your ground," "to stay in the moment," that we might benefit from the discipline.

Often in hard times our goal is to escape the hardship. We want it behind us. But if we recognize the hand of our Father the gardener behind it, we'll ask questions like these: "I wonder what God is pointing out in my life?" "What is He showing me that I need to tend to?" Knowing that trials and hardships come to us from the hand of our heavenly Father, we become more accepting of the difficulty and expectant of God's design for it. Our prayers will take on a different flavor, changing from "Lord, save me from this trial" to "Lord, grow me through this trial."

While the writer of Hebrews uses the expression "endure" in respect to trials, James speaks of remaining steadfast or patient. And he holds out blessing through doing so. "Blessed is the man who endures temptation; for when he has been approved, he will receive the crown of life which the Lord has promised to those who love Him" (1:12).[1] Only by recognizing hardship as discipline will we make the most of the trial instead of making light of it.

Not Valuing It

We make light of God's discipline by not valuing it. It's hard to convince our children that the restrictions we place on them or the consequences we dole out are for their good. Yet, as God's children, we find ourselves in the same place. We bristle. We resist. We even rebel when hardships come

---

1. In this verse, the word *temptation* can also be translated "testing."

to us. Sometimes we join with those who revile God, acting as temperamental teenagers in our selfish pride, thinking we know better (cf. Ps. 139:19–22). Other times we squirm and struggle, like the dog being given its shots by the veterinarian.

However, if we cooperate with God's providence—trusting Him as our Father, confident in His purpose that has brought the adversity to us, expectant of good from it—that mentality changes everything. A classic passage cited at times of difficulty is Romans 8:28: "And we know that all things work together for good to those who love God, to those who are the called according to His purpose." Often we have trouble calling adversity "good." Yet, if we interpret that hardship as discipline, then we see it as constructive to us rather than destructive.

Many times those quoting Romans 8:28 stop there. They don't go on to the rest of the story and so leave Romans 8:28 as a cruel joke without a punch line. Paul tells us the rest of the story in the next verse: "For whom He foreknew, He also predestined to be conformed to the image of His Son." The "all things" that collaborate for "good," including those adversities, come to us with the purpose of conforming us into the image of Jesus.

We see the same sort of goal in the discipline of our Father in heaven. The writer of Hebrews describes its fruit: "Now no chastening seems to be joyful for the present, but painful; nevertheless, afterward it yields the peaceable fruit of righteousness to those who have been trained by it" (12:11). What a remarkable picture! From the turmoil and ferocity of the upheavals of our lives, we can expect an aftermath of the peaceful fruit of righteousness—if we do not make light of the Lord's discipline.

By this discipline expertly tailored to us in our strengths and deficiencies (1 Cor. 10:13), we grow to be partakers of God's holiness. We grow in family resemblance to our only begotten Brother. We experience the result of becoming holy (sanctification), as our Father is holy (1 Peter 1:15).

Let me mention something about *discipline*. Sometimes the word used in the original language is translated "punishment," and other times "instruction." It is the same word used in Ephesians 6:4 where fathers are told to bring their children up in the "nurture and admonition of the Lord." It speaks not just to punishment, but to negative conditions or consequences as part of a discipline framework. Another word we might use to convey the meaning is "train," involving the rigors of sculpting toward a model or goal.

Near where I live is a sprawling public garden called Longwood Gardens, which used to be the estate of a wealthy businessman. He was a conservationist who loved flora and brought in specimens from all over the world. After his death, the estate was opened to the public and has developed over the years into something quite spectacular, drawing visitors from near and far. I find it remarkable to hear the variety of languages being spoken as I walk about. Among the many displays is a topiary garden. It is festooned with large bushes shaped like birds and geometric designs. Those formations did not grow that way. They were carefully trimmed to approximate the desired form.

That's what the discipline of the Lord accomplishes in our lives. Our Father the gardener prunes us. Such pruning is often painful, unpleasant at the time. Yet the result is a thing of beauty—the workmanship of His grace conforming us into the image of His Son in our spiritual development.

Imagine now those topiaries resisting the pruning. They would remain without definition, amorphous. The public would be deprived of their ingenuity. When we make light of the Lord's discipline, we buck against the purpose of God, resisting His training. We adopt a near-sighted approach by rebelling in the moment to the neglect of the bigger picture that faith assures us will result in blessing down the road. Throughout Hebrews 11 we find case studies illustrating this "bigger picture" approach, as that chapter leads into the teaching of Hebrews 12 we have been considering. That bigger picture is Jesus Christ.

Not Heeding It
We make light of God's discipline by not heeding it. This is really the bottom line for us as God's children. He brings such discipline to our lives that we might bear fruit, much fruit, fruit that will last. We are not to ignore or misinterpret the Lord's discipline in our lives. He doesn't want us to miss the fact that God Himself, as our heavenly Father, is an involved parent training us as His children to be holy as He is holy. If we are children of God, we can expect discipline. Now it is incumbent upon us to heed it.

We are reminded in Hebrews 12:12–13 that God's discipline involves helping us to run the race set before us. That race takes into account conformity to Christ in our sonship (in relationship to the Father) and in our servanthood (in service to the Father). Included are fruit of the Spirit and the fruit of a life well lived.

Where, through the adversities of our lives, God reveals to us areas in which we are lacking, or sin impeding our progress, or distractions taking our eyes off Christ, or discouragements slowing us down or sidetracking us, we must take action. Just like concentrated air pressure will expose the weakness of a car's radiator, pressures of life will show us areas of anger, worry, fear, or lack of self-control that we need to address by means of God's wisdom and grace.

How do we go about heeding the discipline of God in our lives and yield ourselves to His personal hand of pruning? Three tactics give us our start.

Submit to it. As Hebrews 12:9 puts it, we are to "be in subjection to the Father of spirits" that we might walk in the way of life (cf. Prov. 7:1–2; 14:12; Isa. 55:1–3). Rather than resist or rebel, we bring our will and desires to serve the purpose of our God.

Scrutinize our lives. How we would want this of our own children! We want them to run with our counsel and take stock of their behavior and attitudes and ambitions. So we must ask what the pressure God exerts is exposing in our hearts. Perhaps here more than ever we need to ask Him to examine our hearts, which can so easily deceive us, and pray with the psalmist:

> Search me, O God, and know my heart;
> Try me, and know my anxieties;
> And see if there is any wicked way in me,
> And lead me in the way everlasting. (Ps. 139:23–24)

A spiritual physical by the Great Physician is in order (cf. Prov. 4:20–27).

One pertinent question as we think of John 15 is, "Lord, how am I not abiding in Christ, and how am I keeping myself from greater fruitfulness?" If abiding is akin to being fully connected to Christ, then we must entreat our Father to open our eyes to self-sufficiency, self-glory, and self-service that challenge that connection and hinder our fruitfulness.

Strengthen ourselves in the grace of God. Though we work out our salvation with fear and trembling, it is God who is at work in us both to will and do for His good pleasure (Phil. 2:12–13). We are His workmanship of grace, building projects of redemption (Eph. 2:10).

We are to be strong in the Lord and the strength of His might. Our ability to endure and press on comes from God. As we wait on the Lord, we will renew our strength, run and not grow weary, walk and not faint (Isa. 40:31).

Sanctification, whereby Christ is formed in us, involves our participation and compliance. But its result as well as its pursuit are by grace, through faith. Apart from Christ we can do nothing. Perhaps this principle is the principal purpose of the Father's pruning—teaching us to abide in Christ.

Cultivating Growth

1. How does the metaphor of our earthly father help us to understand God as our heavenly Father for our spiritual development?

2. How do "weeds" of the flesh compete with and inhibit the growth of the fruit of the Spirit in our lives?

3. In what way is Proverbs 22:6 more of a warning than a promise?

4. How are we to understand the discipline of God?

5. What three ways do we make light of, or "despise," our Father's discipline?

6. What is the rest of the story of Romans 8:28–29 that helps us to understand what "good" refers to?

7. How do Psalm 139:23–24 and Proverbs 4:20–27 lead us in a "spiritual" physical?

Chapter 3

No Ordinary Love

In this the love of God was manifested toward us,
that God has sent His only begotten Son into the world,
that we might live through Him. In this is love,
not that we loved God, but that He loved us
and sent His Son to be the propitiation for our sins.
Beloved, if God so loved us, we also ought to love one another.
No one has seen God at any time. If we love one another,
God abides in us, and His love has been perfected in us.

—1 JOHN 4:9–12

A vine-ripened life looks to the development of the fruit of the Spirit, cultivated by the hand of our heavenly Father in our union with Jesus Christ. As we abide in Christ, remaining rooted and built up in Him, the fruit of new life will grow organically from the inside out. Our lives will take on the character of the One we have been grafted into by grace, taking on the family likeness of our God. As the apostle Paul puts it before he gives his list of the fruit of the Spirit in Galatians 5,

"My little children…I labor in birth again [for you] until Christ is formed in you" (4:19).

That is the goal for which the Spirit is at work—that Christ be formed in us. No family trait is more prominent than the one we find first in the inventory of the Spirit's fruit: love. Just as people will remark about a baby, "He's got his father's eyes," or "She is the spitting image of her mother— just look at her nose," so people will know we are Christians by our love.

But what is love? What does this distinguishing trait of the believer look like? Certainly, the language of love is spoken by the world. Books, movies, and songs contribute to our culture's understanding. Love is a feeling par excellence. People are victimized by it, falling into it like quicksand. Marriages rise as love waxes strong. Divorces follow due to its waning. Immorality is justified in its name. Complete this sentence: Love is _____; you will likely borrow from the world's storehouse for your answer.

Love is a concept shared by secular culture and the church. The question for us is, What does *God* mean by love? How is the fruit of love He cultivates in us as the redeemed of the Lord distinctly Christian? What does love look like that flows out of union with Christ, as an outgrowth of a heart given life by His Spirit? The love our Father would have us exhibit carries at least three distinguishing features.

Birthmark of the Believer
John highlights love as a distinguishing feature of those who have been born again into the family of God: "Everyone who loves is born of God and knows God" (1 John 4:7). Earlier

in his first epistle, John remarks on the origin of this trait: "Behold what manner of love the Father has bestowed on us, that we should be called children of God! Therefore the world does not know us, because it did not know Him" (1 John 3:1).

The comic strip *The Far Side* offered some of the best takes on life as we know it. I remember one *Far Side* cartoon that depicted two deer standing and talking in the woods. One deer had concentric circles on his chest that looked like a target with a bull's-eye. The caption quoted the other deer, who opined, "Bummer of a birthmark, Hal."

Birthmarks can set us apart in good and bad ways. They attract the attention of others and often invite comment. For children of God, a character birthmark is love. Our birthmark is far more providentially serendipitous than Hal's. Yet it also can make us a target—of scorn by those who see it as weakness or of acclaim by those who see it as attractive. Just as the religious leaders saw the boldness of Peter and John and made the connection that they "had been with Jesus" (Acts 4:13), so people are to see an unnatural love in us and make the same connection.

In his first epistle, John highlights this family trait both positively and negatively. On the one hand, he beckons us as true believers to the exercise of love. He calls us "beloved," emphasizing that our very identity is as those loved of God. That's the starting point. We are to love as those who have been loved, are loved, and will always be loved. Nothing can separate us from the love of God bound up in Christ. His love will not let us go.

Having gotten our attention as those who are loved, John expresses our kindred love in positive terms: "Beloved, let us love one another, for love is of God; and everyone who loves is born of God and knows God" (1 John 4:7). We've heard the expression "to know him is to love him." That adage reaches its most profound apex when it comes to loving God. God is love. To grow in the knowledge of God is to grow in love.

Now, translate that to the love of those loved of God. Scripture calls us to love of neighbor, love of the lost, and even love of our enemy (as God so loved us). But John emphasizes here love of others who are beloved of God, fellow believers. The blossoms of love are most abundant and beautiful in the community of God's church. The world is to take notice. Particularly, they are to note a love that is not indigenous to the region. It is decidedly a love from God, scented with the fragrance of grace.

To drive home his point, John reinforces the positive by declaring its negative. "He who does not love does not know God, for God is love" (1 John 4:8). Imagine a family full of musicians. Generations have played a variety of instruments. All have been able to carry a tune. This family is known for its musical prowess. Then along comes Jimmy. Jimmy couldn't carry a note in a bucket. He's not even interested in playing air guitar, and, if he were, he'd somehow produce discordant notes even on that. Knowing his family lineage, what would people ask? "Is that kid actually from that family?"

If love is a dominant trait in our spiritual DNA, then it is a telling sign of our belonging to the family of God. This love is not sedentary. It manifests itself in love for others, as we have been loved and are being conformed to the image of *the* Beloved.

Grace Given and Purpose Driven

They say a picture is worth a thousand words. That's one of the things I like about Facebook. My children post pictures of their children. Cuteness that could not easily be put into words is right there on display. I get to watch the comments build, testifying to the fact and validating my own opinion. Pictures do speak volumes.

What picture would you post to depict love? Would it be Philadelphia's iconic statue by Robert Indiana in John F. Kennedy Plaza (aka Love Park)? That would certainly spell love, but would it show love? Would your picture be something mushy that could find a place on a Valentine's Day greeting card? Or, getting more spiritual, would it be a nice calligraphy of the love passage from 1 Corinthians 13:4–8: "𝕷𝖔𝖛𝖊 𝖎𝖘 𝖕𝖆𝖙𝖎𝖊𝖓𝖙. 𝕷𝖔𝖛𝖊 𝖎𝖘 𝖐𝖎𝖓𝖉.... 𝕷𝖔𝖛𝖊 𝖓𝖊𝖛𝖊𝖗 𝖋𝖆𝖎𝖑𝖘"?

To help us grasp what God means by the word *love*, John pulls out a vivid graphic display: "In this the love of God was manifested toward us, that God has sent His only begotten Son into the world, that we might live through Him. In this is love, not that we loved God, but that He loved us and sent His Son to be the propitiation for our sins" (1 John 4:9–10). John shows us Jesus. He is love incarnate; He is love personified. To understand the love of God, we need to study God's gift of love.

My wife and I just celebrated our anniversary as husband and wife. Our wedding thirty-nine years ago was a testimony to our love. I loved her. She loved me. Our love was mutual, not one-sided.

God's love, however, is a rescue love. He set His love on sinners. Paul explains in his letter to the Romans: "But God demonstrates His own love toward us, in that while we were still sinners, Christ died for us" (5:8). In other words, God set His love on the unlovely, the unlovable, and the undeserving of love. God loved unilaterally as an expression of His grace and saving purpose.

We talk of unrequited love. A teenage boy falls in love with someone out of his league, and his love is not reciprocated. With God we see an "unrequired" love in every respect. He is the one sinned against, spurned by those who bear His image, renounced by those wired for communion with Him. As a holy God, He must punish sin. Instead of justice, however, He shows mercy. Instead of wrath, He lavishes grace. Against all expectations, He gives the Son He loves to die for those who have reviled Him.

The word "propitiation" in the quote that opened this chapter is a telling and chilling word that has to do with wrath. God sent His Son to be the propitiation for our sins—all because of love. The wrath that we deserved as transgressors, guilty and under the sentence of condemnation, was turned aside to the Son of God who stood in our place. On the cross, Jesus figuratively took to His lips the cup of wrath (see Isa. 51:17–21; Matt. 26:39) for our sin and drained it to its dregs, exhausting the wrath of God we deserved—for the sole reason of love.

This is radical love, the sort that distinguishes Christian love from the world's notions of love. It is impossible to grasp the full extent of Christian love apart from the transaction of the cross. Such love defies all sensibilities. It exceeds all expectations.

God's love is the starting point for the fruit of the Spirit we are called to demonstrate. Jesus is our exemplar. We are to love as we have been loved. We emulate the illustration held up for us. We cannot exhibit such love in our natural strength. Love is a catalyst of abiding for the formation of greater love.

Functional versus Sentimental

Don't tell Hallmark, but the love that God has in mind for us as His children doesn't mesh well with their greeting-card line. The love that God wants of us and wants us to cultivate as His children is not some sort of sentimental feeling. He wants us to love in deed—as He has modeled for us in the giving of His Son.

God did not love us merely in word and thought, but in action and intention. God is telling us this love is part of our redemptive makeup. It is to be exercised in our lives, in the strength of the Spirit and the model of Christ.

Such love is to be realized in increasing measure in our character as a mark of maturity in Christlikeness. Demonstration of love in the model of Christ indicates God's love is "perfected in us" (1 John 4:12). What does it mean for God's love to be perfected in us? John explains:

Whoever confesses that Jesus is the Son of God, God abides in him, and he in God. And we have known and believed the love that God has for us. God is love, and he who abides in love abides in God, and God in him.

Love has been perfected among us in this: that we may have boldness in the day of judgment; because as He is, so are we in this world. There is no fear in love; but perfect love casts out fear, because fear involves torment. But he who fears has not been made perfect in love. We love Him because He first loved us.

If someone says, "I love God," and hates his brother, he is a liar; for he who does not love his brother whom he has seen, how can he love God whom he has not seen? And this commandment we have from Him: that he who loves God must love his brother also. (1 John 4:15–21)

Love is perfected in us by abiding in God. Loving others as God loved us is a symptom of that abiding, a telltale sign of our union with Christ as the Vine of life.

What does such love look like? If the love God desires (and the love He requires) exhibits itself in a love for others, how can we recognize it? Again, John shows us Jesus:

By this we know love, because He laid down His life for us. And we also ought to lay down our lives for the brethren. But whoever has this world's goods, and sees his brother in need, and shuts up his heart from him, how does the love of God abide in him? My little children, let us not love in word or in tongue, but in deed and in truth. (1 John 3:16–18)

Just as John 3:16—"For God so loved the world that He gave His only begotten Son, that whoever believes in Him should not perish but have everlasting life"—tutors us in Christian love, so 1 John 3:16 trains us to love in kind. Our love is to be giving, compassionate, and sacrificial—a reflection of how Jesus loved us.

Society understands love in a predominantly sentimental way. Our notion is formed more by Byron, Keats, and Shelley than by the Bible. Often, we are tutored in love by romance novels, TV dramas, and women's magazines. Such love appeals more to the heart than to the mind. We are visceral victims who "fall in love," like a bear into a pit. Our feelings call the shots. Falling in love is a prerequisite to marriage. Falling out of love justifies divorce. "It's not our fault. That's just the way it is," the argument goes.

Biblical love, however, is not governed by the shifting winds of emotions. The love God designs for us can be *commanded* and is itself an expression of obedience. Jesus says, "If you love Me, keep My commandments" (John 14:15–24). Loving the Lord our God with all our being and our neighbor as ourselves is a summary of the law, the Ten Commandments.

The call to love our enemies is not an appeal to generate rosy feelings for those who don't like us, but a call to take action in meeting their needs, despite what they deserve (cf. Luke 6:27–36; Rom. 12:10, 20). To love is not necessarily to like. C. S. Lewis points out that in marriage the husband and wife "can have this love for each other even at those moments when they do not like each other; as you love yourself even when you do not like yourself."[1]

In John 15, where Jesus calls us to a fruitful life through abiding in Him, our Lord highlights love:

> "As the Father loved Me, I also have loved you; abide in My love. If you keep My commandments, you will abide in My love, just as I have kept My Father's commandments and abide in His love. These things I have spoken to you, that My joy may remain in you, and that your joy may be full. This is My commandment, that

---

1. C. S. Lewis, *Mere Christianity* (New York: MacMillan, 1952), 109.

you love one another as I have loved you. Greater love has no one than this, than to lay down one's life for his friends." (John 15:9–13)

We love as we have been loved.

Let me illustrate the power and distinguishing character of Christian love. I have officiated at many weddings over the years. I have a general template for the service, but I work with the couple to make the service their own. They pick out songs and readings and special elements, such as lighting a unity candle. The most requested reading couples select comes from the love chapter of the Bible, 1 Corinthians 13.

Where is that love chapter found? In Paul's letter to the church at Corinth. What do we know about the Corinthian church? It was filled with division. Warring factions jockeyed for acceptance. Paul addresses sexual immorality that "is not even named among the Gentiles" (1 Cor. 5:1). All sorts of doctrinal disagreement pitted the members of the church against one another, creating a party spirit with fortifying factions. An attitude of competitiveness and superiority controlled use of the talents and abilities God had given.

Into this cauldron of acrimony, Paul writes these words:

Love suffers long and is kind; love does not envy; love does not parade itself, is not puffed up; does not behave rudely, does not seek its own, is not provoked, thinks no evil; does not rejoice in iniquity, but rejoices in the truth; bears all things, believes all things, hopes all things, endures all things. Love never fails. (1 Cor. 13:4–8)

The church at Corinth, with all of its infighting and immorality, is not quite the usual setting we hear these words in, is it?

Paul writes to them not in contentment but in conflict, not on the honeymoon but on the verge of divorce! He tells the Corinthians to love with the love of God when their patience is tried; to love those who would rob them of joy; to love when their peace is violated; to love when being kind is the furthest thing from their minds; to love when their record of wrongs spills over to page 3. Such love is triage to marital conflict, not mere garnish to a wedding ceremony. It directs us where to go, according to the need of the moment.

When I minister to people going through marriage problems, I hear a husband who insists that he does love his wife. Rather than leave it there, I'll ask, "Are you being patient with her? Kind? Do you keep a record of wrongs?"

Biblical love brings commitment and responsibility. When a Christian wife vows to love her husband, she doesn't promise to love him only when he's nice or when he loves her as he should. She promises to love as Christ loved her. Capacity to love like that is found only in the Vine and is exercised only by abiding.

Cultivating Growth

1. In what way is love a birthmark of the believer?

2. Why do you think love is first in the list of the fruit of the Spirit in Galatians 5?

3. Whom do the Scriptures call us to love?

4. Where does God direct our attention to give us the clearest idea of the love He expects of us?

5. How does society's conception of love differ from the Bible's?

6. What do John 3:16 and 1 John 3:16 teach us about love?

7. How is the classic love passage, 1 Corinthians 13:4–8, better suited for the conflicts of marriage than for the honeymoon?

Chapter 4

Joy Inexpressible

In this you greatly rejoice, though now for a little while,
if need be, you have been grieved by various trials,
that the genuineness of your faith,
being much more precious than gold that perishes,
though it is tested by fire, may be found to praise, honor,
and glory at the revelation of Jesus Christ,
whom having not seen you love. Though now you do not see Him,
yet believing, you rejoice with joy inexpressible and full of glory.

—1 PETER 1:6–8

I am at the stage of my life when my children are having children. I recently posted a photo on Facebook I entitled "My Quiver's Quiver." The photo shows my wife and me surrounded by our eight grandchildren. Apart from the remarkable feat of getting eight kids, age five and younger, to sit in one place long enough for a picture to be taken, it displayed something else: a reason for joy. In fact, commenters commonly used the word *joy* in response to the photo's posting.

What gives you joy? What image can you conjure that best represents joy? Would you characterize joy as a spectacular thunderstorm that creates plenty of excitement but is fleeting? Or would a more apt image be the dew that covers the ground of daily life—ordinary and even expected? Perhaps the Mona Lisa, with her wry, unwavering smile reflects the steady delight of Christian joy.

This chapter reaches for the produce stand of grace to take hold of joy. Often we experience a withered joy in our Christian lives rather than a plump, ripened joy because we entertain a concept of it divergent from that of Scripture. For us, joy is tied to circumstances, which can be fickle. Therefore, our joy is as ephemeral as is the adrenaline high of good news. In addition, if positive circumstances are the source of joy, how can anyone know such gladness in the face of anxiety, depression, and adversity? If good times are the soil that produces joy, that means a significant portion of our lives is inevitably barren.

Our Father God has something more for us. He wants us to know a joy that belies our circumstances, a joy rooted in the soil of His Son that is always hospitable to fruit production. This chapter examines the joy God has for His children and how that joy can be cultivated.

Joy Explained

Let me again press the question. Answer honestly. What would bring you joy? Perhaps if you came into a financial windfall you would experience joy. Whose mind would not blissfully skip along the path of possibilities at such an occasion? Maybe news that the PET scan shows that your body is cancer free would make you erupt into a fountain of joy. Who would not be overjoyed to hear that the scourge of cancer has been expelled from the body, no longer able to do its damage, no longer a threat to self or family?

I received a request from a friend asking me to pray. His wife had gotten a call following a mammogram that something suspicious had been seen. The doctor wanted to meet with them. Would I pray? You can imagine the thoughts that would lay siege to the mind at such a time.

Later, I received a text from my friend saying all was well. How do you think he felt? He certainly felt relief and, no doubt, joy. But what if the news had not been good? What would have happened to joy then? Would it have withdrawn, like the groundhog seeing its shadow and indicating a long, cold, brutal winter ahead? Would the blooms of joy have lain dormant waiting to be drawn out by the warmth of spring? If we would grasp the joy God has for us, we must firmly position this cornerstone: *the fruit of joy is not rooted in circumstances, but in God's goodness and ultimately in God Himself.*

The apostle Peter was writing to believers scattered and suffering because of persecution. Their situation was oppressive, and their lives were in jeopardy. Peter's counsel is not for them to "hang in there" for a light at the end of the tunnel. Rather, he says this: "In this you greatly rejoice, though now for a little while, if need be, you have been grieved by various trials" (1 Peter 1:6). He doesn't point to joy delayed but joy displayed—right then, in the thick of trial.

What is the "this" in which those enduring persecution are to find joy? Their bliss is rooted in the reality with which Peter opens the body of his letter:

> Blessed be the God and Father of our Lord Jesus Christ,
> who according to His abundant mercy has begotten us
> again to a living hope through the resurrection of Jesus
> Christ from the dead, to an inheritance incorruptible and
> undefiled and that does not fade away, reserved in heaven
> for you, who are kept by the power of God through faith
> for salvation ready to be revealed in the last time. (vv. 3–5)

Rather than in the shifting sands of circumstance, the believers are to find their joy in the unchanging constant of their salvation in the triune God. Peter roots the believers' joy in three established realities.

The Inviolability of Their Inheritance

The people to whom Peter was writing were homeless. More than that, they were hunted. Peter reminds them that while they were not at home, they were not homeless. Because Jesus died and lives for them, they have a home in heaven with Him. They have been born again to a living hope. That hope is the living Christ. They are heirs of eternal life.

Their inheritance is described as "incorruptible and undefiled and that does not fade away, reserved in heaven" for them. I have seen mobile homes covered with decals indicating various places the owners have been. Among those decals I have observed this bumper sticker: "Spending our children's inheritance." That's funny—and it's not, at least for the children whose inheritance is being diminished.

But not only is our inheritance as children of God being kept for us, it is being kept intact. Peter makes that clear by the words and expressions he uses. Our bequest stands imperishable, undefiled, and unfading. All that Christ has laid up for us, every spiritual blessing from His hand, is being guarded by Him in the heavenlies. We will be deprived of nothing.

It's always sad when parents are predeceased by their children. That should not be. But what it means, practically speaking, is that the children will not receive their inheritance. In speaking of the believers' inheritance, however, Peter says not only is the inheritance kept for the Christian, but also the Christian is kept for the inheritance "by the power of God through faith for salvation ready to be revealed in the last time." The full inheritance will be bestowed to all the heirs of grace.

That assured and complete inheritance awaits those who for "a while" (1 Peter 5:10) may have to suffer indignities and injustice at the hands of sinful men—just as Jesus so suffered (1 Peter 2:21). They may be homeless in this world, but they are not homeless in the age to come, which, by the way, is eternal. Eternity imposes itself on today. That is reason for joy!

The Saving Purpose of God

Another reason Peter gives for joy is the saving determination of God Himself. That purpose of God in salvation radically affects our view of life and of self.

Homeless people wrestle with a sense of self-value. Society looks down on them. They are considered outcasts. If you were to call a homeless man "sir," my guess is he wouldn't even look up. He would think you were addressing someone else.

What we call someone carries great weight. How does Peter address those suffering disdain by the world? After identifying himself as an "apostle of Jesus Christ," he, in the name of Jesus, addresses them this way: "To the pilgrims…, elect according to the foreknowledge of God the Father, in sanctification of the Spirit, for obedience and sprinkling of the blood of Jesus Christ: Grace to you and peace be multiplied" (1 Peter 1:1–2).

Not only does God know their predicament, but He also ministers to them in it. The words of grace and peace are not casual pleasantries. They are full of meaning from the mouth of God for those He addresses as His own. "Thus says the Lord"—Father, Son, and Holy Spirit. Even in the trial, the Spirit is at work, growing them in the grace and knowledge of Christ (2 Peter 3:18). They find themselves in their situation as disciples of Jesus Christ, purchased by His blood.

Peter would likely reflect here on his own time with Jesus and the injustices and homelessness He faced. No doubt he would hear his Lord's closing words in Matthew's gospel, urging His disciples to obedience and assuring them of His presence until the end of the age.

The Sanctifying Purpose of God

The writer of Hebrews tells us that it was for the joy set before Him that Jesus endured the cross (12:2). His joy was not in the cross per se, but in what the cross would yield— the acquisition of His bride, the church. Yet the agony of the cross was tinged with joy in that Jesus knew He was willingly carrying out the Father's saving purpose. This is not to diminish the agony, but to point out that adversity does not snuff out the flame of joy. Rather, it fans it in the knowledge of the Father's purpose.

James instructs us to "count it all joy when [we] fall into various trials." Why? He goes on: because we know "that the testing of [our] faith produces" Christlike character (1:2–3).

Jesus knew His suffering had a purpose, the purpose of His Father for Him, and that knowledge stimulated joy in Him. His delight, His food, was to do the will of the Father. And His desire is to stimulate such joy in us through abiding in Him.

Jesus made this clear in His High Priestly Prayer of John 17, the prayer with which He closed His time with His disciples in the Upper Room before heading out to face the cross for which He came. He prayed, "But now I come to You, and these things I speak in the world, that they may have My joy fulfilled in themselves" (John 17:13). Jesus wants us to know His joy and to grow in that joy in ourselves.

One of my favorite places to visit is the highlands of Scotland. The mountains, the history, and the unspoiled beauty create an almost mystical setting. Spread across the moors and glens are purple blankets of heather. The fields of soft wildflowers lend a certain delight to the soul, like the brushwork of God.

Joy is like that. It spreads across the Christian life, bringing beauty to the mundane and the extraordinary. Present in times of peace and times of hardship, it is tended by the hand of our Father in our lives to remind us of His presence, His handiwork of grace that stretches from here into eternity. The hope of heaven colors our world, trials and all.

Without the proper perspective, we can miss out on joy in times of turmoil. Like being obscured by a dark storm cloud, our perspective can be swallowed up so that we see nothing else. But we can also miss out on joy in times of tranquility. In the absence of strife, we lose sight of the hand of our Father God that directs the times of calm and the times of upheaval in our lives.

Joy Expressed

Joy rooted in the Father who adopted us and tends us will thrive apart from the shifting winds of circumstances. The apostle Paul takes this joy and puts it into practice right in the dark situation of his imprisonment: "Rejoice in the Lord always. Again I will say, rejoice!" (Phil. 4:4). Our joy is not in the circumstance but in the One who rules it, whose purpose orchestrates the circumstance and who is at work in it for our good and His glory.

Rejoicing in Joy

The question now is, How do we go about realizing this joy? As we've seen, each of the fruit of the Spirit can be framed as both a noun and a verb, something we see and something we do. In this case, the joy we exhibit is a joy we are to express. Not only are we to consider it joy when we face trials, we are commanded "to rejoice"—always! Commit to memory "Rejoice always," and you will have memorized 1 Thessalonians 5:16. We are to behold and exclaim at the heather adorning the heights and the crags—all the time. It gives life effervescence.

Peter spoke about rejoicing in the wonder and security of our salvation in Christ. His statement "in this you greatly rejoice" links to the living hope of our heavenly inheritance, but also leads us to look to what will fuel joy in us. The settled "in this" of 1 Peter 1:6 prompts the "that" of verse 7 in ongoing activity for us between here and glory:

> that the genuineness of your faith, being much more pre-
> cious than gold that perishes, though it is tested by fire,
> may be found to praise, honor, and glory at the revelation
> of Jesus Christ, whom having not seen you love. Though

now you do not see Him, yet believing, you rejoice with joy inexpressible and full of glory, receiving the end of your faith—the salvation of your souls. (vv. 7–9)

What we see is that joy is cultivated through relationship with Jesus Christ. Our joy is not merely in our inheritance but in the One we long to be with in the inheritance. Jesus makes that clear when He speaks of His preparations for us: "In My Father's house are many mansions; if it were not so, I would have told you. I go to prepare a place for you. And if I go and prepare a place for you, I will come again and receive you to Myself; that where I am, there you may be also" (John 14:2–3).

Joy is nurtured through the exercise of faith in communing with our Lord Jesus. Think of the best joy in your life. Is it things? Certain experiences? Or does the joy of relationship with those you love dwarf the delight of things? Those who find the greatest joy in things lead a cold, sterile existence.

Our joy is in Him who first loved us, the most glorious of all our relationships. Fueling that joy is the knowledge that we were His enemies. He loved us and gave Himself for us as ones who were hideous and hateful in sin. Joy relates to Jesus but is grounded in the contentment of the gospel.

That means one of the ways we incite joy in our hearts is to rest in the gospel, recount its wonders, and recite its truths to ourselves. If your heart grows cold, as it does in certain seasons of life, read the gospel accounts. Remind yourself of who Jesus is and what He did for you. Encounter Jesus anew, breathing life into the cardboard cutout we can make of Him in our religiosity.

Did you notice the remarkable way Peter expressed himself? In the knowledge of Jesus, we are to "rejoice with joy." The realities of our relationship with Jesus, and all that means, are the coals by which we stoke the fire of delight in our Lord.

Road to Joy

How do we get there? How do we find such joy? How do we stoke the flames? How do we stir the embers that trials can threaten to extinguish and that even good times can dampen through neglect of their tending? The primary battleground for joy is the mind. And it is a battle, knowing we have a spiritual enemy who would drive us to diversion, doubt, discouragement, and even despair.

When James tells us to count it all joy when we experience all sorts of trials, he goes on to say, "knowing..." (1:2–3). He calls us to remind ourselves of what we *know*. Paul's letter to the Philippians is called an epistle of joy. Throughout the letter, he uses language related to the mind: "think," "know," "consider," "meditate." After calling us to "rejoice in the Lord always," he goes on in Philippians 4:8 to say: "If there is any virtue and if there is anything praiseworthy—meditate on these things."

Not surprisingly, Peter directs us to the same field of battle to contend with those who would rob us of our joy: "Therefore gird up the loins of your mind, be sober, and rest your hope fully upon the grace that is to be brought to you at the revelation of Jesus Christ" (1 Peter 1:13). The arena for action is the mind.

The weeds of worry and of woe threaten to choke out and obscure the heather of joy. It is through the maintenance of the mind that we uproot those weeds in the soil of our hearts and tend to the glories of grace our God has for us. What does that look like in practice?

Joy on the Job

Joy is realized in the exercise of faith. Faith involves focus on spiritual realities in the renewing of our minds. Two portions of God's Word direct us to His means for our exercise of faith.

The Work of Prayer

Psalm 42 records honest, open interaction with God in the face of threats to joy. We're not going to take time to walk through the psalm in detail, but we can note several features that harken to what we have covered above.

- Joy is found not in circumstances, but in God Himself. The adversities the psalmist experiences precipitate the anguish, but it is the distance he feels from God that plunges him into despair. "My soul thirsts for God, for the living God" (v. 2).

- The psalmist fights against the thieves of joy by remembering. His battleground is the mind: "When I remember these things," he says (v. 4). "O my God, my soul is cast down within me; therefore I will remember You" (v. 6).

- The psalmist does not wallow in his despair; he takes up arms—beginning with his own doubts and fears. His adversaries were laying siege to his joy, but the main problem lay in himself. He was buying into their taunts, their efforts to create doubt (vv. 3, 10) on the existence, presence, and character of his God. So he addresses his own thoughts. He grabs for the reins that he had allowed his enemies to wrest from his hands. He talks to himself:

    Why are you cast down, O my soul?
    And why are you disquieted within me?

> Hope in God, for I shall yet praise Him
> For the help of His countenance. (v. 5)

In fact, this is the refrain of the psalm and its continuation in Psalm 43 (42:11; 43:5).

- The psalmist reminds himself that God remains in charge, and His perfect purposes are at work. God continues as his help (Ps. 43:1–2). These thoughts wipe away the tears of Psalm 42:3 and cultivate joy.

- God is the source of his joy. His truth and light will escort him back to His presence. What will he find there? "The altar of God, to God my exceeding joy" (Ps. 43:4). The joy of his salvation dispels the disorienting fog of unbelief to allow the sun of God's smile to cheer him.

Joy grows in the personal greenhouse of prayer, and it will spread to overrun the heart and adorn the life. That's why when Paul issues the twice-given command "to rejoice in the Lord always," he follows up with a call to prayer and a reference to the mind: "Be anxious for nothing, but in everything by prayer and supplication, with thanksgiving, let your requests be made known to God; and the peace of God, which surpasses all understanding, will guard your hearts and minds through Christ Jesus" (Phil. 4:6–7).

The Perspective of Faith

Coupled with prayer is faith, our second consideration in the cultivation of joy. Faith perceives unseen realities. It interprets life from the truths it believes. It is able to say with full confidence and absolute conviction, "For I consider that the sufferings of this present time are not worthy to be compared with the glory which shall be revealed in us" (Rom. 8:18).

Some of the most remarkable words God has given to help us in the desert of our lives, where joy seems absent, can be found in the book of Habakkuk:

> Though the fig tree may not blossom,
> Nor fruit be on the vines;
> Though the labor of the olive may fail,
> And the fields yield no food;
> Though the flock may be cut off from the fold,
> And there be no herd in the stalls—
> Yet I will rejoice in the LORD,
> I will joy in the God of my salvation.
> The LORD God is my strength;
> He will make my feet like deer's feet,
> And He will make me walk on my high hills. (3:17–19)

We won't approach this portion of Scripture as we did Psalms 42 and 43, but we will highlight a few thoughts to help us cultivate joy in the various soils life brings.

First, in circumstances of distress that inhibit joy, we can issue declarations of faith. We remind ourselves of what we know to be true—by faith. Faith rests in the reality of God and the certainty of His working. Faith trusts, submits, and expects. It is infused with strength for today and bright hope for tomorrow, much as Peter instructed us. When circumstances suggest God is not there or that He does not care, we insist, "I will not base my faith on sight but on His revelation."

Second, circumstances are not the source of our joy. The picture Habakkuk paints is compelling. Though our lives be stripped bare, though our best efforts frustrated, though no relief is in sight, the fountain of my joy cannot be capped. God is my joy. He is my constant. I will rejoice in the Lord—always.

Third, my comfort and strength are not in circumstances, but in the Lord my God. He is my strength and stability. My foot is steady in all terrain of life because He is with me and He is for me. As Nehemiah puts it, "Do not sorrow, for the joy of the LORD is your strength" (8:10). With this knowledge, joy tamped down springs to life and blossoms continually at the tending of our Father the gardener.

Cultivating Growth

1. To what do we typically affix our joy?

2. How does joy differ from happiness? Is there overlap?

3. How can the flame of joy continue to burn in trial rather than being snuffed out?

4. What is our heavenly inheritance, and how can it be a steady source of joy?

5. What does Jesus tell us in His prayer of John 17 about the joy He has in mind for us?

6. How can we cultivate joy in our lives? What role does the mind play in that cultivation?

7. How does Habakkuk 3:17–19 present a picture of joy that is contrary to popular notion and secular thought?

Peace beyond Understanding

Be anxious for nothing,
but in everything by prayer and supplication,
with thanksgiving,
let your requests be made known to God;
and the peace of God, which surpasses all understanding,
will guard your hearts and minds through Christ Jesus.
—PHILIPPIANS 4:6–7

God's Word did not drop from the sky as timeless oracles. Rather, God spoke at many times and in various ways into historical contexts according to the need of the moment. From the driest genealogies to the most fanciful apocalyptic visions, God addresses His people pastorally. He speaks truth—applied.

Over fourteen hundred or so years, through about forty various human authors, God caused His Word to be written down—inscripturated—for the generations to follow. As it was then, so it is now: God's Word is a lamp to our feet and a light to our path (Ps. 119:105). The Scriptures make us wise unto salvation in Jesus Christ and wise for a life lived with and for Him. In them we find what we need for life and godliness.

That makes it easy to write this book on the fruit of the Spirit. All the writings on the subject appeal to the same foundational text—the Word of God. Two parts study, one part experience, structured with a dash of writing acumen produces a helpful volume. However, it's one thing to write a book on a subject. It's quite another to live it.

As a pastor, I have taught from the Bible on the subject of worry. I even wrote an article on it for a theological journal. It was entitled "Worry Unmasked," and it exposed worry for what it is according to our Lord's teaching in the Sermon on the Mount. God has a lot to say on the subject. He knows our frames and frailties and fears. He ministers to us in our need, as He understands that need better than we do ourselves. He does not leave us unprepared.

In addition to teaching on the subject, I have counseled many people struggling with anxiety. I have helped them understand and apply God's counsel to their specific situation. Together we have put the flesh of their problems on the skeleton of God's truth to give them stability and ability to stand and press on.

You would think I would have been prepared.

Peace under Siege

On a Tuesday in early May I sent an e-mail to my congregation from my hospital bed. I had collapsed on the tennis court and been taken by ambulance to the hospital. That would be the entryway to a slew of tests to figure out what had happened to an ostensibly healthy fifty-eight-year-old man.

Before serving the ball, I had put my hands on my knees and complained of dizziness. The next thing I knew, I was strapped to a stretcher hearing the distorted voices of radio communication. Someone said, "I think he's coming around."

Evidently, I had face-planted following my dizziness. That's what concerned the cardiologist. Why had I not just slumped down? Why had I not made any attempt to break my fall? He determined that my heart had gone into ventricular tachycardia at the court, my pulse surging well beyond the capacity of my heart. The cardiologist said 90 percent of those who experience that condition outside of a hospital setting die on the spot. He said I was "very lucky." I replied that I saw it as God's hand of mercy. He paused, thought about that for a moment, and said, "I'll stick with lucky." Clearly, we had a different take on life.

On the tennis court, my tachycardia resolved to the less serious atrial fibrillation, a rapid heartbeat. Whether that was due to the jolt of the fall or the direct hand of God, I don't know. But I do know God's hand was in it. By the time the ambulance got to the hospital, my atrial fibrillation had settled to a regular heart rhythm. But what had happened? That was the question that needed to be answered.

Even though my heart rate had become normal and all other indicators were good, doctors didn't want me to go home from the hospital until the tests had been performed. An echo stress test on Friday showed an irregularity. They wanted to do a cardiac catheterization, which could not be performed until Monday. I had to wait over the weekend with nothing to do—except think.

It was during that time that a tidal wave of anxiety washed over me. I felt like I would drown in it. Has the accelerator of your car ever gotten stuck, causing the engine to race? That's what I felt like, not just in my physical heart but my very being. I can only describe it as a "panic attack," something I had never experienced before. I had lost grip of the reins, and the horses were running amok.

That's when a friend of a friend who worked at the hospital stopped by for a late night visit. I expressed something of my panic to him. His response was calm and nonchalant, quite the contrast to my anxious state. Almost offhandedly, he made reference to God's presence and care. That simple reference acted like the light switch in a dark room, one of those "Why didn't I think of that?" moments. I needed to bring the perspective of God to bear on my situation.

Funny, you would think a pastor would know that. And I did know that. I just wasn't factoring it in for myself. Then it hit me shortly after my visitor left. "I have taught and counseled on worry for years. What have I brought to bear with others that I need to bring to bear with myself?" I had processing work to do.

I turned the page of my mind to Philippians 4:4–8. I had memorized that passage many years ago and was able to work through it as I had done with others. It provided for me a pathway to peace as fruit of the Vine. My Father the gardener met me that evening and restored the anxious arrhythmia of my spiritual heart to normal rhythm. The greater Physician was tending to me.

This chapter charts that pathway to peace along which God led me. The teaching from Philippians puts in place two realities for believers united to Jesus Christ, the Vine of life, the first reality being foundational to the second.

Peace with God

The panic I experienced in the hospital had nothing to do with fear of dying. In fact, when I returned to my church (to attend worship, not yet to preach) weeks after my surgery, someone asked me an unusual question that many would consider inappropriate. It took me aback, but that surprise quickly became delight. He asked me if I was disappointed I did not die. What delighted me was the perspective of faith that he was bringing to bear.

I told him that was a good question, one I had thought about. In fact, earlier in his letter to the Philippians the apostle Paul applies that same perspective. Paul wrote Philippians from prison. He didn't know what the future held, and he knew that he could lose his life. But here is his reasoning: "For to me, to live is Christ, and to die is gain. But if I live on in the flesh, this will mean fruit from my labor; yet what I shall choose I cannot tell. For I am hard-pressed between the two, having a desire to depart and be with Christ, which is far better. Nevertheless to remain in the flesh is more needful for you" (Phil. 1:21–24).

In one sense, death is not the enemy of the Christian. It is an ally. To be absent from the body is to be present with the Lord. Death is gain because it ushers the believer into the very presence of the Lord Jesus. The believer appears before the judgment seat of God without fear and with great joy, already given a verdict of "not guilty" because Jesus was found guilty in his place.

Elsewhere Paul writes that "having been justified by faith, we have peace with God through our Lord Jesus Christ" (Rom. 5:1). In Christ, our sin is atoned for; the debt is paid. The wrath of a holy God upon that sin has been exhausted. Jesus, our substitute, took that cup from our hands and drained it to its very dregs on the cross. In its place, He gives us the cup of blessing from which we drink every time we remember His death at the Lord's Supper.

It is on that basis that we come before God without fear and with exceeding joy (Jude 24). God has reconciled us to Himself in Christ. God "made Him who knew no sin to be sin for us, that we might become the righteousness of God in Him" (2 Cor. 5:21). We are clothed with an alien righteousness, the perfect obedience of the One who arrived at the cross without spot or blemish of sin. I believe that with all my heart. That's why that gentleman's question did not upset me but instead turned my attention to this blessed reality for all those united by grace through faith to Jesus Christ.

The fruit of peace is grounded in the fact of peace. Without that reality of union with Christ, peace is presumptuous. It is no more real or enduring than the relief given through pharmaceutical painkillers that treat the symptoms but not the cause.

When Paul addresses the Philippian church in the salutation of his epistle, he greets them with "grace…and peace from God our Father and the Lord Jesus Christ" (1:2). Those words are not empty sentiment or mere formality. They are rich with meaning. They communicate a reality, the reality of redemptive, reconciled relationship with God the Father through Jesus Christ as Lord.

From that foundational reality flows the fountain of tranquility. It is along this path the Spirit led me to know the peace of God as I walked on the stormy seas of my panic.

Peace of God

I was admitted to the hospital on a Thursday. On Friday I had every test under the sun. I semi-voluntarily gave what seemed like gallons of blood. One of the e-mails to my congregation I signed "Pastor Pincushion."

I was okay amid the flurry of tests. It was during the waiting over the weekend that the walls started to close in. A claustrophobic panic swept over me. It felt like a medicine ball had been placed on my chest. That's when the Lord caught me up through the visit of my friend's friend, when he casually made reference to the peace of God. "Pastor, heed your own counsel," the Lord impressed upon me. With that charge I turned my attention to Philippians 4: "Rejoice in the Lord always. Again I will say, rejoice!" (v. 4).

Where did joy fit in? Answering that question was the first step on the path to peace. I asked myself why I was *not* rejoicing in the Lord. I had no trouble answering that question. The circumstance had obscured my view of God. I was not rejoicing because I was not regarding my Lord. The more I considered, the more I was humbled and convicted by my inattentiveness to the good hand of my God.

That prompted me to give thought to things in which I should be rejoicing. It occurred to me that the reason I found myself in the hospital in the first place was because of God, my Father. His providence had led me to black out. Something was afoot. God was at work. Talk about a perspective transplant! That one fact transformed everything and set me on a radically different course. My thoughts soared to the side of God, escaping the walls of the hospital room closing in on me.

As I let my thoughts explore this new perspective, I took account of evidences of my Father's providence. My tennis partner had the wherewithal to call 911. He turned my head so I would not drown in my own blood. I was at the hospital embarking on a course of discovery that would not have been had the Lord not allowed me to live. He was exposing an insidious invader in my physical heart. All sorts of provisions of His hand presented themselves to my reflection.

As my mind followed this course, my heart was enlarged with praise and appreciation—and anticipation. It made me wonder what more God had in store. How would He be at work in the days ahead?

I turned my attention to the next verse of the passage. "Let your gentleness be known to all men. The Lord is at hand" (Phil. 4:5). I was not alone because God was with me. He wanted me to know that, to embrace that. He wanted me to calm down and consider.

In my stream of consciousness, the Spirit brought other portions of His Word to mind:

> Fear not, for I am with you;
> Be not dismayed, for I am your God.
> I will strengthen you,
> Yes, I will help you,
> I will uphold you with My righteous right hand.
>   (Isa. 41:10)

> Peace I leave with you, My peace I give to you; not as
> the world gives do I give to you. Let not your heart be
> troubled, neither let it be afraid. (John 14:27)

I meditated on these passages, savoring their truth. They
were like honey to the soul, and my eyes brightened. My
heart was nourished and strengthened. The enemy of peace
was pushed back.

Then came the sobering words: "Be anxious for nothing,
but in everything by prayer and supplication, with thanksgiving, let your requests be made known to God" (Phil. 4:6). I
had to talk with my Father about my fears. I had to tell Him
about my failure of faith. I did believe and asked Him to
help me in my unbelief. "Prayer," "supplication," "requests"—
clearly, my Father wanted me to cast my cares on Him,
knowing He cares for me.

Seasoning it all, like salt to food, was thanksgiving. Knowing my God's presence and providence and perfect purpose
colored everything. Just as I had gained reason for rejoicing, I
found grist for giving thanks. If they had been drops of water,
the things that occurred to me would have spilled over the rim
of the cup. My soul was refreshed. My cup runneth over.

The more I followed this path, the more prominent the
"peace of God, which surpasses all understanding" became for
me. Against the interloper, the enemy of my soul, this peace
took its position as a sentry, guarding my heart and mind in
Christ Jesus.

It is clear that the battleground for the prize of peace is
the mind. That's why the apostle turns from speaking of the
mind in Philippians 4:7 to the assignment of verse 8: "Finally,
brethren, whatever things are true, whatever things are noble,

whatever things are just, whatever things are pure, whatever things are lovely, whatever things are of good report, if there is any virtue and if there is anything praiseworthy—meditate on these things."

This verse served as a deadbolt to secure the door of my heart and keep anxiety at bay. I turned my thoughts to the various elements listed. The point was not to engage in mere positive thinking, like some sort of exercise in naive optimism about the seriousness of the situation. Rather, the point was to bring my mind to dwell on profitable things, things that drew me more deeply into the arms of my Father God, things that would fortify me with His truth and console me with His providence.

The destination of the journey along the path was not simply peace, not even the peace of God. It was the God of peace. As Paul concludes the section in verse 9, "The God of peace will be with you." The prize of peace that stands at journey's end, like the proverbial pot of gold at the end of the rainbow, is grounded in the Prince of Peace who has been with us all along. In our panic, we lose sight of Him who is our shalom. The peace that surpasses understanding is simply a return to take refuge in that realization.

The "Rest" of the Story

Peace comes from resting in God. It knows His presence and trusts in His providence. It submits to His will, and it resides in His Son.

My cardiac catheterization revealed diffuse cardiac disease. Evidently, I had a family history, only I didn't know my family well enough to know that (which is another story). I needed multiple bypass surgery.

I wrote an e-mail to my congregation, alerting them to what was going on and asking them for prayer. Here's a portion of that e-mail.

> I have struggled, but God has brought me to rest in His will. As you've heard me say before, a trial is a weight room for the exercise of faith. The Holy Spirit is our trainer, knowing how much we can bear and just what our needs are (to conform us to Christ).

I then pointed them to the passage I have shared with you.

> The passage that's given me the greatest direction is Philippians 4:4–8. Trials and uncertainty provide unique settings in what it means to rejoice in the Lord "always," not to be anxious about "anything," in "everything" to give thanks. God's path to His peace in this passage has been precious to me and has helped me to focus on His presence and His cornucopia of blessings and wisdom.

My Father, the gardener, had tended to me. He had shored up my faith against my own fear and against the attacks of the devil. It's interesting that the weekend lull had been a down time in the hospital, but the Spiritual Physician had been on duty attending to me.

We are reminded here of the active nature of abiding. We need to bring the peace of Christ to bear in life's trenches. We need to apply God's Word to our lives, being not only hearers but practitioners of it. In those trenches the fruit of the Spirit displays particular beauty and vigor.

Cultivating Growth

1. In what way is peace *with* God foundational to the peace *of* God?

2. Why can a Christian have peace in the midst of upheaval?

3. What place do God's presence and providence play in finding peace?

4. How do Isaiah 41:10 and John 14:27 bring us a peace unknown to unbelief?

5. What role does the mind play in finding peace?

6. How does prayer lead the way in knowing the peace Paul describes?

7. To what ultimate destination does the path of peace lead us?

Chapter 6

The Leaven of Patience

For this reason we also, since the day we heard it,
do not cease to pray for you,
and to ask that you may be filled with the knowledge of
His will in all wisdom and spiritual understanding;
that you may walk worthy of the Lord, fully pleasing Him,
being fruitful in every good work
and increasing in the knowledge of God;
strengthened with all might, according to His glorious power,
for all patience and longsuffering with joy.
—COLOSSIANS 1:9–11

Eternity could be defined as "the period of time between when the traffic signal turns green and the person at the front of the line of cars decides to go." At least that's what an impatient person might think.

Even to speak of an impatient person raises questions and concerns. Are there those who are naturally patient and those temperamentally not so? Should we be patient with impatient people because that's just the way they are? Should we excuse our own impatience for the same reason? Often when people decry a lack of patience in themselves, they say it with a chuckle. It's not that big an issue—certainly not on a level with other fruit of the Spirit, right?

My word-processing program's thesaurus offerings serve as an exegetical expositor of the perils of impatience and, conversely, the importance of patience. My cursor hovers over *impatient* and the following are suggested as synonyms: annoyed, edgy, irritated, intolerant, exasperated, aggravated, irked, and piqued. These alternatives do a good job displaying the danger of impatience. It is malware to the soul.

One of our challenges in understanding patience is to see its potency and potential as a deal breaker for cultivation of the other fruit of the Spirit: little patience, little rest of the fruit. What if Jesus had been loving, gentle, and kind, but not patient? What impact would that have had on the whole?

We cannot but be impressed with Jesus' patience. He would spend an entire day surrounded by hoards of people clamoring for His attention. He would teach them and heal their ailments. Then, spent from the day's labors, Jesus would withdraw for rest and solitude in prayer. Yet the crowds tracked Him down. Jesus would look upon them and be moved with compassion.

I know when I've labored long in the ministry of the day, the last thing I want is for my phone to ring and to be called out to service. Yet Jesus thought not of Himself but of the sheep. His compassion was laced with patience that put others' interests before His own. Rather than being annoyed, His heart for the Father's will drove Him.

Patience is not merely a social grace. It is a driving force for growing us in the character of the Vine. In this chapter we explore patience, probing its spiritual composition. With that understanding we move to its practice, bringing it to the helm of decisions and direction.

Patience Profiled

How would you define *patience*? We could take all those synonyms for *impatience* from my word-processing program's thesaurus and turn them on their head to get a good feel for what it is. We might observe that patience is something exhibited in the face of an irritant, like the person at the front of the line when the traffic light turns green. Perhaps "potential" irritant would be a better way to put it. Certainly, our Lord Jesus did not allow the demands of the crowd to dampen His patient compassion.

Behind the sense of patience is a fuse. We might think of a stick of dynamite. The explosive charge awaits, but the fuse to get there can be short or long. Some people have a short fuse before they blow up. Patience suggests a long fuse.

God is never impatient, but His patience is not without limit. We see His patience tested in the rebellion of His people throughout the Old Testament. Peter informs us that the Lord is "longsuffering toward us, not willing that any should perish but that all should come to repentance" (2 Peter 3:9). Paul speaks in Romans 2 of God's patience regarding sin. Romans 3:25 defines it as His "forbearance," whereby He stayed His hand of judgment while awaiting His Messiah. The psalmist describes God in this way: "But You, O Lord, are a God full of compassion, and gracious, longsuffering and abundant in mercy and truth" (Ps. 86:15). (The Greek translated here as "longsuffering" can also be rendered "patience" or "endurance.") God is patient, but that patience is not infinite. There will come a day when His wrath will be discharged, as typified in the exile of ancient Israel. However, God is *slow* to anger.

The heart of patience is not tolerance, not even perseverance. It is just what we see in our Lord Jesus, who regarded others more important than Himself. In Philippians 2 Paul doesn't label that something for us. He does reference love (v. 2), so that is at least part of the equation. He also contrasts this something that was in Jesus with "selfish ambition or conceit" (v. 3). He identifies humility as a driving force behind patience (v. 3).

This analysis helps us to see what triggers impatience in most of us. Impatience is the thorn bush that grows in the soil of pride. Pride is all about us—our desire, our preference, and our convenience reside at the center of our universe. Others revolve around us. When people don't do *what* we want, *when* we want we react with irritation—sometimes contained in resentment and bitterness, sometimes expressed in rage and venom.

I live in a development off a busy road. Despite traffic signs to the contrary, people speed. That presents a challenge pulling out from my development into the flow of traffic. Even when I am in that flow ready to turn off that road to go back home, I need to be careful. I will put on my right turn signal well in advance, and still the driver behind me may rush up to my car and lay on his horn. Evidently, I had interfered with his early arrival at the next traffic light. Road rage is impatience in the extreme. To say to the driver cut off in traffic, "Why not rather be wronged?" is to speak a foreign language.

Impatience is full of self. Patience is low on self. Impatience is fueled by pride. Patience is driven by the application of love.

Patience seems to be the cocktail to all the other fruit of the Spirit, with love as the base and the other fruit lending the various flavors of grace. Let me show you what I mean by way of contrast in regard to the other fruit.

- Impatience has self at the center. Patience is driven by love that denies self and puts others first.

- Impatience is barren of joy. Patience approaches adversity or inconvenience while considering it all joy to encounter the trial.

- Impatience leads the assault on peace. Patience rests in God's hand of providence and so is seasoned with thankfulness.

- Impatience breeds unkindness. It can be decidedly mean-spirited. Patience shows mercy.

- Impatience practices evil and inflicts harm. Patience puts goodness on display to the glory of God and benefit of neighbor.

- Patience exhibits faithfulness, gentleness, and self-control. Impatience fosters the opposite, promoting discord, strife, and those deeds of the flesh that are contrary to the fruit of the Spirit.

Like regulated blood pressure is an indicator of good health, patience with strangers, our spouse, and our children is a telltale sign of how well the other fruit of the Spirit are developing in our lives. If our patience is lacking, we can be sure the other fruit are underdeveloped.

The nature of patience is a willingness to suffer. It will endure inconvenience, injustice, and irritants. It suffers long. We see that in our Lord Jesus: "For to this you were called, because Christ also suffered for us, leaving us an example, that you should follow His steps: 'Who committed no sin, nor was deceit found in His mouth'; who, when He was reviled, did not revile in return; when He suffered, He did not threaten, but committed Himself to Him who judges righteously" (1 Peter 2:21–23).

I think we can safely say the driver who rushed up on my tail and laid on his horn when I tried to turn into my development was impatient. But if we could turn the tables, the issue of the moment was not him, but me. The example given by our Lord Jesus would have me focus on how I handled the situation. How did I manage my attitude in terms of love, joy, peace, gentleness, and self-control in my patience with others? Such assaults on our patience reveal what needs to be done in the cultivation of the fruit of the Spirit in our lives. The question is, How does our God direct us in the practice of patience by abiding in the Vine?

Patience Practiced

If we were to pick out one Bible character to illustrate patience, it would likely be Job. As Samson is associated with strength, Job is linked to patience. James holds him up as an exemplar of the fruit, saying, "You have heard of the perseverance of Job" (5:11). It is interesting to note James couples the patience of which Job is an example with suffering (5:10). Together with the prophets, he is blessed as those who steadfastly "endure." The word in the original is different from that of Galatians 6, but it belongs to the family of patience, helping us to understand it. In fact, the term James uses carries the same root as "abide" in John 15, a sort of hyper-abiding.

How was Job a paragon of patience? It certainly couldn't mean he did not sin or even that he did not show impatience. The Job who said, "Shall we indeed accept good from God, and shall we not accept adversity?" is the same Job of whom it is said, "In all this Job did not sin with his lips" (Job 2:10). It is the same Job who would later complain, protest his innocence, and demand an answer from God in chapter 31.

But what we see in Job is a man who exhibited steadfast endurance in the face of suffering, and unmerited suffering at that. He maintained his faith perspective. That perspective served as the basis for his wrestling and perseverance—and his responsiveness to the rebuke of God.

How can we cultivate such patience in our lives? The same way Job did. Against the hounding words of his counselors, Job uttered this confession of faith:

> For I know that my Redeemer lives,
> And He shall stand at last on the earth;
> And after my skin is destroyed, this I know,
> That in my flesh I shall see God,
> Whom I shall see for myself,
> And my eyes shall behold, and not another.
> How my heart yearns within me! (19:25–27)

Job's persistence was grounded in the hope of the gospel.

The gospel is the generator to patience. Without its redemptive influence, our efforts at patience can amount to little more than gritting our teeth. We grin and bear it. Without the gospel, our effort will take on more of a negative feel than positive. That's what makes patience more than a social grace. It is a trait cultivated more by sanctification than socialization. It flows from a Christ-centered hope. It follows a Christ-centered model.

We've seen how impatience tends to be self-centered and self-serving. The gospel turns that around. As God has treated us, so we will treat others. A richer understanding of the gospel will displace us at the center with Jesus. It will seek to serve rather than be served.

The gospel reprograms us to treat people not in a way they deserve but as an exercise of grace and mercy. Reflect on all those times we turn our back on God to follow after sin. Think of how often we have asked our Father for forgiveness for the same sin. Consider how often we have dishonored His name and neglected His will. Why does God put up with us? The answer is, His grace in the gospel where our sin was laid on Jesus. That grace trains us to go and do likewise. That means the way our God has dealt with us becomes the power and pattern for our dealing with others. Patience fuels forgiveness and forbearance.

James gives us helpful counsel for the practice of patience when he says we are to be "swift to hear, slow to speak, slow to wrath" (1:19). But why? James goes on to tell us that "the wrath of man does not produce the righteousness of God" (1:20). The point of reference is not our vindication, but the validation of the righteousness of God in our lives. God becomes the point of reference, not us. The target affects our aim. The goal determines our game plan.

Patience becomes the pause button to take stock of whether our reaction will promote the righteousness of God in itself and in the eyes of others. I need to challenge myself that when someone cuts me off in traffic and I respond unseemly, does my response promote righteousness? How many of us have been chagrined by inappropriate behavior only to notice someone we know looking on?

Our actions either honor or dishonor God, and they lend counsel to others. One time I parked in a parking garage. A large van nestled beside me. When I returned to my car to leave, I edged out ever so gently because my vision was obscured by the van. A man and his daughter (I presumed), maybe seven years old, emerged from behind the van into my view. I stopped abruptly. No harm was done. You couldn't tell that by the man's reaction. He flew into a rage, reaming me out for my reckless driving. I was surprised he didn't physically assault my car or even me.

What occurred to me was that this was the way the man was teaching his daughter to deal with conflict. Others watch us. The fruit of patience asks us if our behavior promotes righteousness. Do others take measure of our behavior and give glory to our Father in heaven? Would we want the scene memorialized on YouTube?

One other note about the practice of patience. The verses that opened this chapter make patience a matter of prayer. Paul prays for the Colossians that they might "walk worthy of the Lord, fully pleasing Him, being fruitful in every good work." He asks that they may be "strengthened with all might, according to His glorious power, for all patience and longsuffering with joy" (Col. 1:10–11).

We must pray for patience in our own lives. We need to pray for one another in the same regard. The production of fruit will come through abiding in the Vine. Apart from Christ our efforts will be fruitless. So we pray. And we pray. We stumble and we pray still more. The power comes not from ourselves but from Christ, as Paul makes clear by his reference to our transfer from the bondage of sin to the kingdom of Christ, through the gospel of freedom (Col. 1:13–14).

James would have us pray for wisdom from above to know God's guidance for exegeting our situations and applying His truth. The wisdom he unpacks sounds quite amenable to patience: "But the wisdom that is from above is first pure, then peaceable, gentle, willing to yield, full of mercy and good fruits, without partiality and without hypocrisy." The end product for those who sow peace and not disorder is the "fruit of righteousness" (3:17–18).

Perfected by Patience

Life serves as a proving ground for patience. It is definitely learned on the job rather than simply in the classroom.

The Pink Panther films of the 1960s and 1970s featured a bumbling French police detective named Inspector Jacques Clouseau. After a full day of stumbling obliviously toward unwarranted success, Inspector Clouseau would return home, where he lived with his manservant, Cato. One of Cato's responsibilities was to lay in ambush, ready to launch a surprise attack on the good inspector. The idea was to keep Clouseau on his toes.

Our lives are filled with Cato encounters, those events that spring up to test our patience. Will we respond with grace or wrath? Growth in Christlikeness will have us increasingly respond in grace. The more real the gospel becomes in our lives, the more relevant it will become in our encounters with others and the more the character of our Messiah will be realized in our dealings—in all its fruit.

In the face of a spiritual enemy who would stoke the flames of pride that burn within each of us, we want to rest in the strength of our God and revel in His love. Let Paul's words of welfare lead us to abide in the Vine for fruitfulness of new life in Christ: "Now may the Lord direct your hearts into the love of God and into the patience of Christ" (2 Thess. 3:5).

Cultivating Growth

1. How would you define *patience?*

2. How do we see patience displayed in Jesus?

3. What fuels impatience? What promotes patience?

4. In what way does patience contribute to the other fruit of the Spirit?

5. Why is Job an example of patience for us and an encouragement to us in our impatience and complaining?

6. How is the gospel a generator of patience?

7. How does God use "Cato moments" to cultivate the fruit of patience in our lives?

Not-So-Random Kindness

But God, who is rich in mercy,
because of His great love with which He loved us,
even when we were dead in trespasses,
made us alive together with Christ
(by grace you have been saved), and raised us up together,
and made us sit together in the heavenly places in Christ Jesus,
that in the ages to come He might show
the exceeding riches of His grace in His kindness
toward us in Christ Jesus.

—EPHESIANS 2:4–7

I had mixed feelings about dropping my son off at college for his freshman year. On the one hand, that was the way it was supposed to be. We raise our children to leave the home and start a life of their own. College is a major mile marker in that journey. God had led the way to open that door for him.

On the other hand, there was the emotional trauma of my youngest child leaving the nest, creating a hole in our home and in my heart. I knew in my mind that he would be coming home for breaks and we'd be in regular communication, but still there was grieving.

Evidently, Grove City College understood this trauma. When we arrived, along with many other first-year students, we were met at the freshman dorm with the smiling faces of white-shirted upperclassmen. Emblazoned across their shirts were the words "Orientation Board." When we pulled up to the door, members of the OB swarmed the car and quickly unloaded its contents.

The OB is a group of over a hundred students who are well versed in separation anxiety and the practical needs of college freshmen. They have a slew of events planned to ease the transition. Their web page gives this greeting: "We have been praying for you since before you were even accepted, and we'll continue to do so well after we meet you in person."

That sensitivity to need and practical expression to meet it is what kindness is all about. This chapter explores the fruit of kindness, both as a character of the King and a characteristic of His kingdom.

Kindred Kindness

Kindness is not an exclusively Christian commodity. In fact, we can see something of all the fruit of the Spirit manifested in people and communities across the globe. As image bearers of God, human beings reflect God's character. His common grace squelches the evil that could be and cultivates in people a care for others that makes this world a delightful place in which to live.

We recognize kindness among our fellow men. When my daughter Sarah was born, doctors discerned a sound in her heart that should not have been. We were referred to a pediatric cardiologist. It turned out she had a heart murmur that didn't appear to be serious, but did merit keeping track of. The doctor thought it might close up on its own as she grew, but it might require surgery down the road. She would need regular checkups and would need to take precautions, such as getting an antibiotic before dental work.

Sarah was born when I was in seminary. We had no money or insurance. The cardiologist knew that and charged us the whopping amount of nothing—nothing for his service or for all the echocardiograms performed in his office. Nothing. But you couldn't tell we weren't paying anything from the way he treated us. He was attentive and unrushed. He cut no corners when it came to caring for my little girl. As far as I know, that physician was not a believer. But he was certainly kind, showing a kindness of which the godliest individual would be envious.

I've heard kindness described as a "constant readiness to help." It not only sees a need, which in itself is significant, it also acts to meet that need. Christian kindness does so in the model of our Savior and at His mandate. John speaks of such kindness as an assurance of faith and expression of love:

> By this we know love, because He laid down His life for us. And we also ought to lay down our lives for the brethren. But whoever has this world's goods, and sees his brother in need, and shuts up his heart from him, how does the love of God abide in him? My little children, let us not love in word or in tongue, but in deed and in truth. (1 John 3:16–18)

Kindness is the hands of love, with the mind of Christ.

The word for kindness carries the sense of benevolence, usefulness. It implies action suitable to or appropriate to a need. Paul clarifies kindness (in this verse translated "goodness") by contrasting it with severity in Romans 11:22: "Therefore consider the goodness and severity of God: on those who fell, severity; but toward you, goodness." Kindness is not harsh, but helpful. As an expression of the gospel, it does not treat people as they deserve, but on the basis of compassionate care.

Kindness pulsates through the burden bearing of Galatians 6: "Brethren, if a man is overtaken in any trespass, you who are spiritual restore such a one in a spirit of gentleness" (Gal. 6:1). While gentleness is singled out as the "how" to bear the burden, kindness can be identified as the "why." How many times in our lives have we been in trouble of our own making, even to the point of being caught in it, like a foot in a bear trap? Yet our parent or a friend has bailed us out or gone to bat for us.

That's how kindness works. It takes stock of others. It is not self-centered. Upon seeing, it acts to meet the need. Such kindness could range from a cheerful word or a comforting arm to opening the door for someone whose hands are full, to giving up a week to dig a septic tank on the mission field, or to spending a day helping a friend move into a new home.

Kindness is a common grace but should be especially verdant as a fruit of the Vine, expressive of sanctification. Such kindness grows from the soil of grace, reaches to the welfare of others, and climbs toward the light of the glory of God.

Christian kindness is an essential feature of every testimony of saving faith. The kindness of God factors large in explaining how we find ourselves engrafted into the Vine. As recipients of kindness, we are to be responders in kindness.

Ephesians 2:1–10 presents the theological template behind personal stories of conversion. It unfolds in three chapters: a backstory (vv. 1–3); God's intervention of grace (vv. 4–9); and new life in Christ (v. 10). Prominent in chapter 2 is the display of "the exceeding riches of [God's] grace in His kindness toward us in Christ Jesus" (v. 7). We defined kindness in terms of selflessly regarding the needs of others and acting in practical ways to meet those needs. How much more glaring is this in the kindness of God expressed to us!

We were dead in sin, without hope and without God in this world. The shackles of sin held us. The sentence of condemnation hung over us, awaiting the just wrath of a holy God. Yet God, in His mercy and grace and love, had compassion on us. He sent His Son to take our sin upon Himself that the Father might take us to Himself. No longer are we children of wrath, but now children of life.

On that trek to the grave, verse 7 highlights that God met us at a point of desperate need, in a predicament of our own making, and displayed the wonder and glory of His kindness. The immeasurable riches of His grace bound up in Christ came to us gift-wrapped in the splendor of His kindness. And that kindness continues to the coming age, when God has even more to show us of its vastness. Our present peace and relief are but a taste of what is yet to come.

What does this kindness look like among the community of the redeemed? We could flesh it out through all the "one another" passages of the New Testament that describe for us the body life of the church. We can get a salient flavor of the fruit of kindness in respect to the destroying effect of sin in the body: "Therefore, as the elect of God, holy and beloved, put on tender mercies, kindness, humility, meekness, longsuffering; bearing with one another, and forgiving one another, if anyone has a complaint against another; even as Christ forgave you, so you also must do" (Col. 3:12–13). Kindness conspires along with other fruit of the Spirit to thwart the efforts of the evil one to divide. As a strong breeze, it circulates the winds of the gospel, refreshing the people of God with its healing message of peace. But the kindness of the gospel belongs not just to the community of faith; it reaches out to communicate the presence of Christ.

Kingdom Kindness

People being kind to people—that is kindred kindness. We see it among those in the world, a product of God's common grace. Through it we bless one another. How do you feel when someone is kind to you? A commercial shows one person holding the door for another person. It brings a smile to her face. She in turn picks up a package an older gentleman dropped. He smiles and does likewise when the opportunity presents itself. I don't remember the product being advertised, but I do remember the smiles evoked by the acts of kindness and the message that kindness is contagious.

Kindness is different for Christians. It takes on a redemptive character, both in us and in the world around us. It could well be called "incarnational compassion." We become the face and hands and feet and voice of Christ to others. Kindness becomes a calling card we extend on behalf of the kingdom of God, representative of the King Himself.

As believers, we have been delivered from the domain of darkness and transferred to the kingdom of Jesus (Col. 1:13). The distinctive and distinguishing behavior related by Jesus in the Sermon on the Mount speaks to that transfer. We are different from those of the world. We are different from the most strident of religious types. Our allegiance is to Jesus Christ, an allegiance that flows from the inside out in a heart occupied by our Lord.

At the core of that sermon in Matthew 5–7 stands the model prayer our Lord taught to His disciples. That prayer bids us to beseech our Father for the advancement of His kingdom. At the chapter's end, Jesus lays out the priority of seeking first the kingdom of God and His righteousness (Matt. 6:33). Kindness plays a special role in our prayer and practice as God's instruments for kingdom advancement.

We labor in this world for the sake of Christ and the service of His kingdom. Kindness is one way for us to represent Christ to others, both believers and unbelievers. As Jesus said in Matthew 5:16, we are to let our light shine before others that they may see our good works and glorify our Father in heaven. Perhaps they will take note of our behavior and ask us to give reason for the hope we have. But even if they do not, we will have still been able to bless them with deeds of kindness.

Jesus was a miracle worker. He turned water into wine, gave sight to the blind, and enabled the lame to walk. He even raised the dead. He performed these miracles not as a sideshow but to show the presence and nature of the redemptive kingdom.

From prison John the Baptist sent emissaries to Jesus, asking Him if He was the expected Messiah. Jesus replied by pointing to His message and miracles: "Jesus answered and said to them, 'Go and tell John the things which you hear and see: The blind see and the lame walk; the lepers are cleansed and the deaf hear; the dead are raised up and the poor have the gospel preached to them'" (Matt. 11:4–5). Miracles were manifestations of the messianic kingdom. They reversed the destructive effects of the fall, giving evidence that the kingdom of God had come with the person of the King.

God still does miracles, but the signs and wonders of the apostolic era have ceased as normative. While we are not endowed with the ability to perform miracles as were Peter and Paul, we can bring relief to the burden of a fallen world through acts of kindness. We can ease their load of life and cheer them with the love of Christ.

In the final of the five teaching blocks in the gospel of Matthew (chapters 24–25), Jesus speaks of the end of the age. He talks about His coming again, the day or hour of which no one knows. He relates the parable of the ten virgins, five foolish and unprepared and five wise and ready, in view of His appearing. He tells the parable of the talents, urging His followers to responsible stewardship of all He has entrusted to them in this life. And then Jesus comes to the scene of final judgment.

Jesus as the Son of Man in His first appearing did not come to judge, but to be judged. But at His return He will judge all peoples. Two doors loom large. One is the door to freedom and eternal life. The other is the door to the bondage of eternal punishment.

The verdict is not pronounced at this judgment. The people of the world are already identified as sheep or goats. They don't become sheep or goats in that scene. Sheep are those for whom

Christ came, those given Him by the Father, those for whom He died. The goats are those who have not bowed the knee. They refuse to recognize the Messiah and so stand unrighteous, condemned. They have rejected the gospel by which they could live.

Jesus already knows the sheep. He is not meeting them for the first time. He knows them—by name. They know Him. He holds them fast in His hand. He will not lose one of them. He has prepared a place for them where they might be where He is forever.

Jesus knows the sheep, but how do we, as readers and onlookers, recognize them? Jesus explains:

> "'For I was hungry and you gave Me food; I was thirsty and you gave Me drink; I was a stranger and you took Me in; I was naked and you clothed Me; I was sick and you visited Me; I was in prison and you came to Me.' "Then the righteous will answer Him, saying, 'Lord, when did we see You hungry and feed You, or thirsty and give You drink? When did we see You a stranger and take You in, or naked and clothe You? Or when did we see You sick, or in prison, and come to You?' And the King will answer and say to them, 'Assuredly, I say to you, inasmuch as you did it to one of the least of these My brethren, you did it to Me.'" (Matt. 25:35–40)

We know them by the fruit of kindness, as evidence of God's handiwork of grace in their lives. As Jesus was accredited as Messiah by His words and deeds, so we are accredited as His subjects by words and deeds that emulate Him.

Not-so-Random Acts of Kindness

We've likely seen the bumper sticker "Practice Random Acts of Kindness." We can't help but fantasize what the world would be like if more people took that challenge to heart. In our more introspective moments, we may feel chastised by it as something we should do in earnest as followers of Jesus.

But for us, acts of kindness should not be characterized by the arbitrariness of randomness. As the white-shirted students of the Orientation Board at Grove City College made kindness their job, so should we. We must be intentional. Kindness is something we should be armed with each day in our foray through the paths of life. We want people to see Jesus.

Only by abiding in the Vine can we conduct this business of the kingdom. We want to study our Lord, whose disciples we are and whose life we are to emulate. The mercy and love and grace that compelled Him must compel us who have tasted of them. As we decrease and He increases, the cause of kindness will flow naturally and necessarily.

Incarnational compassion is the kingdom agenda of kindness. The students of the OB anticipated the nervousness, the fears, and the feelings of isolation of freshmen leaving their families and entering a world foreign to them. And they took practical actions to relieve those fears and help the rookies take their first steps into a new phase of life. That kindness ministered to my son and the other freshmen. And, I can tell you, it ministered to the parents of those freshmen as well.

The fruit of kindness not only adorns our lives with Christlikeness; it also sweetens a world reeling under the effects of sin. It introduces this world to the age to come. It carries an agenda, taking into account a need and acting to meet that need. Our Father Himself sets the bar for us in the kindness He has shown us by meeting our deepest need through the giving of His Son, that we might not perish but have everlasting life.

Let us pray in this fashion that we might cultivate kindness through abiding in the Vine:

Heavenly Father, who has bestowed such kindness on us in Your Son who loved us and died for us, we ask three things of You. Grant us an increasing awareness of Your kindness to us in delivering us from the bondage of sin and establishing us in Your eternal kingdom. Make us alert to opportunities that surround us each day by which we can be the face and hands and feet and voice of Christ to others. Use us as agents of compassion, relieving the burdens of others, cheering them on their way, pointing them to Jesus, Your Son, our Savior. Amen.

Cultivating Growth

1. How is kindness displayed through God's common grace?

2. What words would you use to describe the character of kindness?

3. How do we approach everyday living with an agenda of kindness?

4. How is God's kindness to us a model and motive for our kindness to others?

5. How does the expression "incarnational kindness" get to the heart of kindness as a fruit of the Spirit?

6. What parallel is there between the miracles of Jesus and our acts of kingdom kindness?

7. How is kindness in evidence in the judgment scene of Matthew 25:35–40?

Chapter 8

Gracious Goodness

Let him who is taught the word share in all good things
with him who teaches.
Do not be deceived, God is not mocked;
for whatever a man sows, that he will also reap.
For he who sows to his flesh will of the flesh reap corruption,
but he who sows to the Spirit will of the Spirit reap everlasting life.
And let us not grow weary while doing good,
for in due season we shall reap if we do not lose heart.
Therefore, as we have opportunity, let us do good to all,
especially to those who are of the household of faith.

—GALATIANS 6:6–10

It's not unusual to see writers and commentators address goodness together with kindness in treatments of the fruit of the Spirit. Certainly, there is overlap between the two. But if God in His wisdom has separated them out for us in His inspired Word, then it is incumbent upon us to give them separate treatment, to discern the differences.

What is goodness? Anyone who has ever had teenage offspring in the house has probably heard the words, "I'm starving. What's for dinner?" What they mean is that they are hungry, perhaps very hungry. But they likely are not starving, which would mean that their body is eating itself away because there are no calories to sustain it. In the same way, we can use the term *good* and have only a vague notion of what the trait entails.

Are we to think in terms of behavior, being "good" and being "bad"? In that case goodness would be more akin to righteousness than kindness.

Perhaps we are to think along the lines of good deeds, like those a Boy Scout would do as part of each day's agenda. Included in Scout paraphernalia is a Good Turn Coin. On the front are the Scout emblem and the words, "On my honor I will do my best." The reverse side includes the instruction, "Secretly transfer me to your right pocket each day after your good turn has been done." That would align more with the understanding of kindness laid in the previous chapter. There we saw kindness as taking account of a need and taking practical steps to meet that need. In this sense, a good deed could be more proactive than reactive.

A Good Model

The best place to start in getting a handle on goodness is to see it in the One in whose likeness we are to grow. As a flamingo takes on its pink color from the carotenoids in the algae it consumes, so we take on the character of the Vine in which we abide. Luke records an encounter in his gospel that leads us to do a double take.

> Now a certain ruler asked Him, saying, "Good Teacher,
> what shall I do to inherit eternal life?" So Jesus said to
> him, "Why do you call Me good? No one is good but
> One, that is, God. You know the commandments: 'Do
> not commit adultery,' 'Do not murder,' 'Do not steal,'
> 'Do not bear false witness,' 'Honor your father and your
> mother.'" And he said, "All these things I have kept
> from my youth." So when Jesus heard these things, He
> said to him, "You still lack one thing. Sell all that you
> have and distribute to the poor, and you will have trea-
> sure in heaven; and come, follow Me." (18:18–22)

You may be thinking, "Wait! What? Is Jesus saying that He is
not good? Or is He saying He is not God?"

Neither—Jesus was challenging the ruler's view of
goodness. He turned to the standard by which goodness is
measured and held it up as a mirror for the ruler to examine himself. Like Narcissus the hunter in Greek mythology,
the ruler looked at his reflection and saw everything flawless.
Not a hair of righteousness was out of place. No doubt the
ruler gave a look of self-satisfied smugness. His résumé of
righteousness made him eminently qualified for eternal life, at
least so he believed.

Having gotten the ruler on the same page of the Ten
Commandments, Jesus pulled the rug out from under him.
Pressing the last commandment not to covet, Jesus bade the
young man to jettison his possessions and follow Him where
he would find true riches.

Alas! The ruler did not measure up to God's standard of
goodness. He was not qualified. The standard was the goodness of God Himself. That was the goodness required to
inherit eternal life.

By saying that only God was good, Jesus was not saying He was not good or not God. Rather, He was challenging the ruler's anemic, external, self-obtainable concept of goodness. Like so many, the ruler thought himself worthy of eternal life because of his obedience, his conformity to the law of God. He had the right standard, but he held a superficial understanding of it.

We are reminded of our Lord's teaching in the Sermon on the Mount. There Jesus took the Pharisees to task for their deficient view of righteousness and inadequate understanding of the law. He instructed His disciples: "For I say to you, that unless your righteousness exceeds the righteousness of the scribes and Pharisees, you will by no means enter the kingdom of heaven" (Matt. 5:20).

Jesus then goes on to illustrate that the righteousness God requires applies not only to the prohibition but also to the requirement of the commandments, and not only to behavior but also to the heart:

> "You have heard that it was said to those of old, 'You shall not murder, and whoever murders will be in danger of the judgment.' But I say to you that whoever is angry with his brother without a cause shall be in danger of the judgment. And whoever says to his brother, 'Raca!' shall be in danger of the council. But whoever says, 'You fool!' shall be in danger of hell fire....
>
> "You have heard that it was said to those of old, 'You shall not commit adultery.' But I say to you that whoever looks at a woman to lust for her has already committed adultery with her in his heart." (Matt. 5:21–22, 27–28)

In His interaction with the ruler, Jesus was making clear the deficiency in the man's understanding of the law and his insufficiency in respect to righteousness. The apostle Paul spells it out in his primer on the gospel in Romans 3:19–24.

> Now we know that whatever the law says, it says to those who are under the law, that every mouth may be stopped, and all the world may become guilty before God. Therefore by the deeds of the law no flesh will be justified in His sight, for by the law is the knowledge of sin.
>
> But now the righteousness of God apart from the law is revealed, being witnessed by the Law and the Prophets, even the righteousness of God, through faith in Jesus Christ, to all and on all who believe. For there is no difference; for all have sinned and fall short of the glory of God, being justified freely by His grace through the redemption that is in Christ Jesus.

The goodness of the gospel is expressed in terms of the righteousness of the law. Only that righteousness will qualify for entrance into heaven. It is gained not by works but by grace alone, through faith alone, in Christ alone (see Eph. 2:8–9).

Jesus helps us to understand goodness by pointing us to God. The law exposes our lack and need. It points us to Christ as God's provision of the garment of goodness by which we are outfitted for eternal life. But the fruit of goodness speaks to more than righteousness.

Our Lord leads us to a firmer grasp of goodness by holding up for us another portrait of God as good. In Matthew 20 Jesus relates a parable of workers hired for labor in a vineyard. The landowner recruits laborers throughout the day, from early morning to the eleventh hour. He offers the fair daily wage of a denarius. When it comes time to pay the workers, he gives all of them the same wage, to the confusion and consternation of those employed earlier in the day (and no doubt the hearers of His parable). Jesus' point is made in the interaction between the first group hired and their employer for the day:

> "And when they had received it, they complained against the landowner, saying, 'These last men have worked only one hour, and you made them equal to us who have borne the burden and the heat of the day.' But he answered one of them and said, 'Friend, I am doing you no wrong. Did you not agree with me for a denarius? Take what is yours and go your way. I wish to give to this last man the same as to you. Is it not lawful for me to do what I wish with my own things? Or is your eye evil because I am good?'" (Matt. 20:11–15)

The word translated "good" in verse 15 is sometimes expressed as "generosity," but it has the same root as the word in Galatians 5 translated "goodness." The employer is asking the workers, "Do you begrudge my goodness?"

In the parable, Jesus is illustrating grace. The parable's point is not about what is earned but what is unearned. The wages were dispensed at the discretion of God without regard to merit. The working arrangement was a setting for the display of God's gracious goodness.

Jesus shows us that the goodness expected of us in respect to the character of God features two traits. One, it conforms to the ethics and standards of a good God. Two, it is linked to freely given generosity. The fruit of goodness flows from grace, expresses grace, and follows the contours of God's workmanship of grace.

So how do we demonstrate goodness in the model of our Father in heaven? Do we behave ourselves because Santa Claus is coming to town and we want to make sure we are on the nice list and not the naughty one? Does our goodness merit us something or put God in our debt?

No, we gain goodness by emptying ourselves of any goodness that we think dwells within us and finding our goodness in God alone. That is no small task. As C. H. Spurgeon said in his inimitable way in a sermon on the Beatitudes: "Our imaginary goodness is harder to conquer than our actual sin." Christ is our goodness. We live out the goodness our God wants of us in following Jesus Christ in a life of obedience that emulates the model of our Father's gracious generosity.

We take on the character of the Vine in which we are rooted by grace. "God alone is good." Our Father tends us to bear that fruit. Peter speaks of it as being "partakers of the divine nature" (2 Peter 1:4), the outflow of which is a fruit-filled life, part of which is a peculiar goodness.

> His divine power has given to us all things that pertain to life and godliness, through the knowledge of Him who called us by glory and virtue, by which have been given to us exceedingly great and precious promises, that through these you may be partakers of the divine nature, having escaped the corruption that is in the world through lust.
>
> But also for this very reason, giving all diligence, add to your faith virtue, to virtue knowledge, to knowledge self-control, to self-control perseverance, to perseverance godliness, to godliness brotherly kindness, and to brotherly kindness love. For if these things are yours and abound, you will be neither barren nor unfruitful in the knowledge of our Lord Jesus Christ. (2 Peter 1:3–8)

Designed for Goodness

An elderly father came to visit his son and his family. He planned to stay a week. One morning at breakfast the father asked his son if he had a newspaper. The son sighed heavily and said, "Dad, get with the times. Newspapers are old school. Everything you want you can find right here with my iPad." The father paused and give a slight shrug of the shoulders. Taking the iPad from his son's hand, he slowly turned and smacked the fly that had been bothering him.

Things are designed for a particular purpose. God states that His design for those He granted new life in Christ is for good works. Paul spells that out in two places: "For we are [God's] workmanship, created in Christ Jesus for good works, which God prepared beforehand that we should walk in them" (Eph. 2:10). "Our great God and Savior Jesus Christ…gave Himself for us, that He might redeem us from every lawless deed and purify for Himself His own special people, zealous for good works" (Titus 2:13–14).

Paul is not bidding us to put on tights and a cape and embark on a quest of good works. He is describing ordinary life lived for Jesus Christ, life expressive of the Vine into which we have been grafted by God's grace. As such, our lives are fragrant to God, ourselves, and others with the aroma of grace.

Notice in Titus 2:14 that goodness is contrasted with lawlessness. Lawlessness refers to making ourselves the arbiter of good and evil. It is doing right in our own eyes (see Judg. 21:25) not merely to earn salvation but to rule our own lives. In coming to Christ, however, we bow before Him as Lord of our lives. We submit our will to His and seek His agenda, as He did to the Father.

John addresses this conformity to Christ in his first epistle. He defines sin as lawlessness and shows the fruit of abiding in Christ: "Whoever commits sin also commits lawlessness, and sin is lawlessness. And you know that He was manifested to take away our sins, and in Him there is no sin. Whoever abides in Him does not sin. Whoever sins has neither seen Him nor known Him" (1 John 3:4–6). "Goodness" refers to the life of the redeemed, those who have turned from idols to serve the true and living God. It speaks to a new orientation to life and a new ambition, expressed in new obedience, exercised through abiding in Christ (see 1 Cor. 15:10; Col. 1:29).

The psalmist gives us an idea of what this new orientation to life looks like. First, he would have us experience the goodness of God:

> Oh, taste and see that the LORD is good:
> Blessed is the man who trusts in Him!
> Oh, fear the LORD, you His saints!
> There is no want to those who fear Him. (Ps. 34:8–9)

The parallel of verses 8 and 9 suggests that the fear of the Lord is the fountain of goodness.

Fear of the Lord is not so much being afraid of God as it is affirming a right view of Him. It gives Him the proper place, the glory due His name. In so doing, it adopts for itself a posture of service, submission, and obedience.

According to the psalmist, this fear can be learned. "Come, you children, listen to me; / I will teach you the fear of the LORD" (Ps. 34:11). One of the lessons we are taught is the "good" life.

> Who is the man who desires life,
> And loves many days, that he may see good?
> Keep your tongue from evil,
> And your lips from speaking deceit.
> Depart from evil and do good;
> Seek peace and pursue it. (Ps. 34:12–14)

A life that operates in the fear of the Lord is a life that flows out in goodness. It leads to the sort of good works "prepared beforehand" that we should walk in them. It flows out in the good works for which we are now zealous by God's workmanship of grace.

Anyone who has planted zucchini or tomatoes knows how prolific these plants can be. In the same way, our Father tends us to be bountiful in savory goodness. Jesus' parable of the soils in Mark 4 makes clear that good soil produces good fruit, whether it be thirtyfold, sixtyfold, or a hundredfold.

A Good Return

There is one other aspect for us to consider in God's design for our goodness. We have seen that God's goodness is expressed in terms of gracious generosity. That is exactly what Paul explains to the Galatians:

> Let him who is taught the word share in all good things with him who teaches. Do not be deceived, God is not mocked; for whatever a man sows, that he will also reap. For he who sows to his flesh will of the flesh reap corruption, but he who sows to the Spirit will of the Spirit reap everlasting life. And let us not grow weary while doing good, for in due season we shall reap if we do not lose heart. Therefore, as we have opportunity, let us do

good to all, especially to those who are of the household of faith. (6:6–10)

We are called to sow goodness. Our Lord gives us an agenda of good.

Fruit holds the seeds of its own propagation. After enjoying an apple, we can take the seeds at the core, dry them, germinate them, and plant them. That strategy pertains to the fruit of the Spirit as well, including goodness.

Paul describes doing good in terms of *sharing* what God has given us. As God has blessed us with time or possessions, we do good by sharing these with others. In so doing, we sow God's grace in their lives as it has been sown in ours. Paul applies this principle in his second letter to the Corinthians, one time in terms of means and the other in terms of mercies.

Blessed be the God and Father of our Lord Jesus Christ, the Father of mercies and God of all comfort, who comforts us in all our tribulation, that we may be able to comfort those who are in any trouble, with the comfort with which we ourselves are comforted by God. (2 Cor. 1:3–4)

But this I say: He who sows sparingly will also reap sparingly, and he who sows bountifully will also reap bountifully. So let each one give as he purposes in his heart, not grudgingly or of necessity; for God loves a cheerful giver. And God is able to make all grace abound toward you, that you, always having all sufficiency in all things, may have an abundance for every good work. As it is written:

"He has dispersed abroad,
He has given to the poor;
His righteousness endures forever."

> Now may He who supplies seed to the sower, and bread
> for food, supply and multiply the seed you have sown
> and increase the fruits of your righteousness, while
> you are enriched in everything for all liberality, which
> causes thanksgiving through us to God. (2 Cor. 9:6–11)

Notice the way it works. We are blessed to be a blessing. We
are to be conduits of God's grace that has come to us. We sow
by sharing. We will reap what we sow.

Galatians 6:10 tells us to be opportunistic in doing good
to others, especially fellow believers, and especially the local
family of believers to which we belong by virtue of church
membership. Those who have vowed to give themselves to the
work of the church should hear these words next time a plea
goes out for nursery workers for church functions.

What would a reputation for good works look like? Paul
tells Timothy in describing the older widow that she has a
reputation "for good works:…has brought up children,…has
lodged strangers,…has washed the saints' feet,…has relieved
the afflicted,…has diligently followed every good work"
(1 Tim. 5:10). Christ Himself is our model and mandate (see
2 Cor. 8:8–9). We might think of sowing good deeds as a
kingdom investment. Through it we lay up treasure in heaven.
Paul urges not to grow weary in so doing (Gal. 6:9).

Johnny Appleseed was legendary, but he was not legend.
Living in the early 1800s, Johnny, whose real name was John
Chapman, embarked on a mission of planting apple seeds to
allow for the westward expansion of the United States. By our
good deeds we can extend the kingdom of God as others see
our good works and bring glory to our Father in heaven.

Peter certainly saw goodness as an armament of the kingdom and an introduction to the gospel. The good deeds of the believer could prompt others to ask the reason for that behavior. We are to be good not for goodness's sake, but for the sake of God our Father. Peter's theology of suffering is capped with a call to goodness: "Therefore let those who suffer according to the will of God commit their souls to Him in doing good, as to a faithful Creator" (1 Peter 4:19).

Cultivating Growth

1. What was the lesson on goodness that Jesus was impressing on the ruler in Luke 18?

2. How is goodness akin to righteousness and kindness?

3. What does our Lord want us to understand about the goodness He requires of us, according to Matthew 20:11–15?

4. How does Psalm 34 lead us in the cultivation of goodness?

5. In what ways does our goodness reflect God to others?

6. How does goodness function as both sowing and reaping in Galatians 6:6–10?

7. What relationship is there between goodness and good works?

Chapter 9

A Great Faithfulness

He who is faithful in what is least is faithful also in much;
and he who is unjust in what is least is unjust also in much.
Therefore if you have not been faithful in the unrighteous mammon,
who will commit to your trust the true riches?
And if you have not been faithful in what is another man's,
who will give you what is your own?

—LUKE 16:10–12

Over the twenty-five years I have served in my present pastorate, I have had the privilege of officiating at many weddings. I find all the preparation that can go into the event astounding! As a pastor I see the hubbub from a distance, but when my daughter got married I got to see it up close and personal. It seemed that every day for eighteen months there was some detail that needed attending to.

But when all the bluster of the ceremony is stripped away, the wedding boils down to one simple element—faithfulness. The couple exchanges vows to strive with one another through thick and thin, till death separates them from one another.

The groom pledges his troth, the bride hers. Only something out of their control will relieve them of the responsibility of their solemn oath, and that is death.

Faithfulness, however, is not fashionable in our day. People go back on their word all the time. We look at Hollywood marriages. Often, the bride and the groom get married so many times the pastor could do a sermon series for their weddings. That shows the low regard our society has for marriage today. It particularly bears witness to the flimsiness of faithfulness.

While fidelity may not be fashionable among those of the world, it is indispensable for us who bear the name of Jesus Christ. As we are a people of the Word, so we should be a people of our word. This fruit pervades the pages of Scripture, both in positive portrayal and negative display. In this chapter we will sample the fruit of faithfulness, seeing it exhibited in our God and then seeing how it is expected in us.

Our Faithful God

There are a lot of extreme things out there today: extreme sports, extreme makeovers, extreme couponing. *Extreme* means "greater than ordinary." It suggests radical, excessive, even unreasonable. That's how we want to look at the faithfulness of God. God is faithful beyond reason, faithful in the extreme.

The Old Testament shows us a promise-making, promise-keeping God. He entered into a promise-laden relationship with Abraham called *covenant*. The history of Israel can be sketched along the lines of faithfulness. It chronicles a faithful God who is true to His word and an unfaithful people who constantly go back on theirs. They turn away from God to follow the idols of the nations around them. They commit spiritual adultery. The prophets who call them to account use some pretty graphic language to call it what it is (e.g., Ezek. 23:16–21). Yet God perseveres in His faithful love, as the book of Hosea illustrates.

The low point in Israel's history has to be when Jerusalem was destroyed and its people deported to Babylon. The books of 1 and 2 Kings employ Deuteronomy, the book of the covenant, as a lens by which the deportation is explained. Time and time again the people had rejected the words of the prophets (Deut. 13, 18). They had rebelled against God in setting up altars to false gods, or even to the true God in places other than Jerusalem, where He would cause His name to dwell (Deut. 12). The verdict was that the prophets, priests, kings, and people had been unfaithful. They had broken covenant.

Yet amid the flames and rubble of a ravaged Jerusalem, the prophet Jeremiah writes these words:

> This I recall to my mind,
> Therefore I have hope.
> Through the LORD's mercies we are not consumed,
> Because His compassions fail not.
> They are new every morning;
> Great is Your faithfulness....
> For the Lord will not cast off forever.
> Though He causes grief,
> Yet He will show compassion
> According to the multitude of His mercies.
>   (Lam. 3:21–23, 31–32)

God proved faithful to His word of warning, and He would be faithful to His word of promise.

Why was God so unreasonable by keeping His promises? Why would He find a place for compassion, room for steadfast love? After all, if someone wants nothing to do with us there comes a point when we say, "Okay, if that's the way you want it." Why is God so stubborn, so unwavering in keeping His promises?

We find two answers stemming from one reason. One, God cannot lie. The writer of Hebrews explains the surety of God's promise to Abraham, and thus to all believers: "that by two immutable things, in which it is impossible for God to lie, we might have strong consolation, who have fled for refuge to lay hold of the hope set before us" (Heb. 6:18). Two, God cannot violate His character. Paul writes:

> If we are faithless,
>   He remains faithful;
> He cannot deny Himself. (2 Tim. 2:13)

The theme of faithful love turns the page for us to the New Testament, in new covenant fulfillment and realization of promise. The Hebrews text goes on to encourage us to put our trust and find our hope in Christ in the assurance of God's faithfulness (6:19–20). Jesus is the only one faithful to the covenant demands, and it is in Him that God keeps His promises. In the book of Revelation, Jesus, as the Redeemer King, is portrayed in faithfulness. He is the faithful witness (1:5; 3:14). His very name is "Faithful" (19:11).

Like a skeleton of steel rebar reinforces concrete, so the faithfulness of God upholds us in our lives as Christians. A sampling makes the point.

- We bank on God's faithfulness for our salvation (1 Cor. 1:8–9).

- We trust in God's faithfulness for our protection against temptation and the tempter (1 Cor. 10:13; 2 Thess. 3:3).

- We look to God's faithfulness for our forgiveness when we confess our sin (1 John 1:9).

- We are sustained by God's faithfulness in our pilgrimage in this world as we wait for glory (1 Peter 4:19).

- We persevere in the knowledge of His faithfulness that undergirds our hope (Heb. 10:23).

- We cling to God's faithfulness as He walks with us along the uneven terrain of life in a fallen world. The Psalms are filled with allusions and specific references to this (e.g., Pss. 5:7; 13:5; 25:6–7; 26:3).

Faithful to Faithfulness

United to Jesus Christ, in the Vine of life, we are called to exhibit the hardiness of faithfulness that is characteristic of our Lord. In one sense, the heart of our relationship with God can be put in terms of our faithfulness to Him.

Fidelity relates to the very essence of discipleship. We pledge our troth to Jesus, vowing to deny ourselves, take up our cross, and follow Him. Bowing before Him as Lord of our lives, we adopt His tone of "not my will, but Your will be done." We give ourselves over to the agenda of His kingdom, living in His ethics, values, and priorities that distinguish us from the world.

What does faithfulness look like in our lives? It starts with being faithful to ourselves. At first blush that sounds like something out of pop psychology: "Be true to yourself." But God's call to us is to be true to who we are *in Christ*, true to our *redeemed* selves. We are to take on the characteristics of the Vine in which we find our life and new identity.

The apostle Paul challenges us to be true to our *new* selves. Notice his reasoning:

> And you He made alive, who were dead in trespasses and sins, in which you once walked according to the course of this world, according to the prince of the power of the air, the spirit who now works in the sons of disobedience, among whom also we all once conducted ourselves in the lusts of our flesh, fulfilling the desires of the flesh and of the mind, and were by nature children of wrath, just as the others....
>
> This I say, therefore, and testify in the Lord, that you should no longer walk as the rest of the Gentiles walk, in the futility of their mind....
>
> For you were once darkness, but now you are light in the Lord. Walk as children of light. (Eph. 2:1–3; 4:17; 5:8)

Paul describes us in terms of a before and an after. He speaks of the intervention of God in our lives to bring us from death to life. Then he issues a call for us to live accordingly. This is what theologians call the *indicative* and *imperative*. The fact requires and regulates the command.

At the start of Ephesians 4, Paul bids us to live in a manner worthy of the calling with which we have been called. Every admonition of the epistles is predicated upon our union with Christ and God's handiwork of grace in our lives. Our new lifestyle presupposes new life: "Therefore, if anyone is in Christ, he is a new creation; old things have passed away; behold, all things have become new" (2 Cor. 5:17).

We might express our call to be true to ourselves in Christ as integrity. *Integrity* means "being whole, together." Sometimes when fire has ravaged a building, a city inspector will condemn it, saying it has lost its structural integrity. As Christians, integrity means being faithful to who we are in Christ. It means uncompromising, relentless allegiance to our Lord Jesus, unmitigated and unwavering in our commitment to Him. The rubber of faithfulness meets the road of life in the way we conduct ourselves. At home, at work, and in our neighborhoods we are to exhibit consistency of Christlike character.

In His parable of the shrewd manager, Jesus contrasts faithfulness with dishonesty: "He who is faithful in what is least is faithful also in much; and he who is unjust in what is least is unjust also in much." To be faithful is to be trustworthy (Luke 16:10–11).

The parable calls our attention to how we are handling what our God has entrusted to us. Integrity of life will show up in how we handle our money, how diligently we work, and how dependable we are in relationships. We are to be honest before God and neighbor, people to be trusted and relied upon.

A major way this integrity manifests itself is in our word. It is startling how little people's word means nowadays. They no longer even need to cross their fingers behind their back. Their word comes with an "if" and a "maybe" built right in, even in the most solemn of vows.

As disciples of Jesus we are to let our yes be yes and our no be no. Faithfulness as a fruit of the Spirit leads us to be true to our vows to Jesus to follow Him, true to our vows to church membership, true to our vows to our spouse, wherever we have made a pledge (see Eccl. 5:2–5). Like a rusty bolt, we should refuse to budge. That sort of determination will require resolve and sacrifice, things in short supply in our self-serving age.

Faithfulness in Action

Dr. Robertson McQuilkin was president of what was Columbia Bible College and Seminary in South Carolina from 1968–1990. His wife, Muriel, was his partner in ministry for many years. She supported her husband in all the entertaining that goes along with the role of college president. In her own right, Muriel was a well-respected, nationally known speaker and radio host. Then something changed. Dr. McQuilkin talked about it in a February 2004 interview with *Christianity Today*. The following excerpts give us the gist. I encourage you to find the interview on the Internet to read all of it.[1]

> It has been a decade since that day in Florida when Muriel, my wife, repeated to the couple vacationing with us the story she had told just five minutes earlier. *Funny*, I thought, *that's never happened before*. But it began to happen occasionally.
>
> Three years later, when Muriel was hospitalized for tests on her heart, a young doctor called me aside. "You may need to think about the possibility of Alzheimer's," he said. I was incredulous....

---

1. Robertson McQuilkin, "Living by Vows," *Christianity Today*, February 1, 2004, http://www.christianitytoday.com/ct/2004/februaryweb-only/2 -9-11.0.html.

Muriel never knew what was happening to her, though occasionally when there was a reference to Alzheimer's on TV she would muse aloud, "I wonder if I'll ever have that?" It did not seem painful for her, but it was a slow dying for me to watch the vibrant, creative, articulate person I knew and loved gradually dimming out....

I approached the college board of trustees with the need to begin the search for my successor. I told them that when the day came that Muriel needed me full-time, she would have me. I hoped that would not be necessary till I reached retirement, but at 57 it seemed unlikely I could hold on till 65. They should begin to make plans. But they intended for me to stay on forever, I guess, and made no move. That's not realistic, and probably not very responsible, I thought, though I appreciated the affirmation.

So began years of struggle with the question of what should be sacrificed: ministry or caring for Muriel. Should I put the kingdom of God first, "hate" my wife and, for the sake of Christ and the kingdom, arrange for institutionalization?...

People who do not know me well have said, "Well, you always said, 'God first, family second, ministry third.'" But I never said that. To put God first means that all other responsibilities he gives are first, too. Sorting out responsibilities that seem to conflict, however, is tricky business.

In 1988 we planned our first family reunion since the six children had left home, a week in a mountain retreat. Muriel delighted in her children and grandchildren, and they in her. Banqueting with all those gourmet cooks, making a quilt that pictured our life, scene by scene, playing games, singing, picking wild mountain blueberries was marvelous. We planned it as the celebration of our "fortieth" anniversary, although actually it was the thirty-ninth. We feared that by the fortieth she would no longer know us.

But she still knows us—three years later. She cannot comprehend much, nor express many thoughts, and those not for sure. But she knows whom she loves, and lives in happy oblivion to almost everything else.

She is such a delight to me. I don't have to care for her, I get to. One blessing is the way she is teaching me so much—about love, for example, God's love. She picks flowers outside—anyone's—and fills the house with them....

I wrestled daily with the question of who gets me full-time—Muriel or Columbia Bible College and Seminary....

When the time came, the decision was firm. It took no great calculation. It was a matter of integrity. Had I not promised, 42 years before, "in sickness and in health...till death do us part"?...

As I watch her brave descent into oblivion, Muriel is the joy of my life. Daily I discern new manifestations of the kind of person she is, the wife I always loved. I also see fresh manifestations of God's love—the God I long to love more fully.

I don't include this account to say there is only one option for dealing with a loved one beset by Alzheimer's. I don't include it even to say anything about marriage. I lay it before you as an illustration of faithfulness that holds concern for God at its core. Such faithfulness displays a determined love, an unwavering commitment, and a sacrificial heart. It is true to its word. It is tenacious; we might even say pigheaded. And, we must admit, such faithfulness is attractive and reassuring to those who look on.

Let me close this chapter with a benediction prayer for the grace we need to display such tenacity of character. It reminds us that the cultivation of the Spirit's fruit in the character of Christ rests in the hand of our Father, the gardener, who works in us both to will and to do according to His good pleasure:

> Now may the God of peace Himself sanctify you completely; and may your whole spirit, soul, and body be preserved blameless at the coming of our Lord Jesus Christ. He who calls you is faithful, who also will do it. (1 Thess. 5:23–24)

Cultivating Growth

1. How would you evaluate the faithfulness of our day?

2. How does God display faithfulness in respect to His covenant?

3. What are some of the ways we experience God's faithfulness in our lives?

4. What part does faithfulness play in our relationship to Jesus as His disciple?

5. What does it mean to be "true to self" as an expression of integrity in our union with Christ as the Vine?

6. How does faithfulness reflect the conduct of the whole of our lives—from our stewardship, to our work, to our word?

7. What features of faithfulness are exhibited in the comments of Dr. McQuilkin?

Chapter 10

Gentle Strength

*Come to Me, all you who labor and are heavy laden,
and I will give you rest.
Take My yoke upon you and learn from Me,
for I am gentle and lowly in heart,
and you will find rest for your souls.
For My yoke is easy and My burden is light.*

—MATTHEW 11:28–30

I think we could use a line from one of today's famous comedians to describe gentleness. It "gets no respect." Jerry Bridges notes: "We pray for patience, we pray for love, we pray for peace and self-control. But who of us ever prays for the grace of gentleness?"[1]

How many times have you confessed your sin of not being gentle with others to God? We confess our lack of love or lack of kindness, but rarely do we admit before God our deficiency in gentleness. It just doesn't make the list. If it does, it's like the boy left standing after all the others have been picked for

---

1. Jerry Bridges, *The Fruitful Life* (Colorado Springs: NavPress, 2006), 141.

one side or the other in a pickup basketball game. It's recognized because it has to be, but it doesn't really have anything to contribute.

This slighted fruit even has identity issues. One translation will say "meekness" and another, "gentleness." It gets even more muddled when we are told in Titus 3:2 "to speak evil of no one, to be peaceable, gentle, showing all humility to all men." Guess which word is the fruit in question? It's not the one translated "gentle." It's the one translated "humility"!

Yet that very coyness of gentleness lends it an air of mystery that spurs probing. God, in His wisdom, includes gentleness on a list of the Christlike character traits the Holy Spirit is working in us as sons and daughters of the living God. This gentleness is not merely a social grace that differentiates us from those who are crude or rude. Rather, it is a sanctifying grace that distinguishes us from who we were prior to union with Christ. We begin our exploration of the fruit by looking at the epitome of manhood, Jesus Christ.

The Gentleness of Jesus

Consider how Jesus describes Himself: "Come to Me, all you who labor and are heavy laden, and I will give you rest. Take My yoke upon you and learn from Me, for I am gentle and lowly in heart, and you will find rest for your souls. For My yoke is easy and My burden is light" (Matt. 11:28–30).

This is one of the passages I've always cherished. I was introduced to it and committed it to memory in my early days as a new believer in Christ. Jesus invites us who are worn out and weighed down to come to Him and find rest. Notice He doesn't say, "I am the One who controls the winds and seas—come," or "I am the One who can heal the sick and raise the dead—come." Rather, He beckons us to Himself with the winsome tone of gentleness and humility. We can't help but feel drawn to Jesus. It's like He is opening His arms to receive us in our weariness.

I am a tennis player and fan. I watched the opening match of the US Open, the last major tournament of the season. Two women took the court in the sport's largest venue, Arthur Ashe Stadium. On one side was Serena Williams, the number one player in the world. On the other was Francesca Schiavoni, the unranked opponent selected by virtue of the draw. Schiavoni was no match. She had trouble getting points, let alone games. It must have been a mortifying experience. At one point in the match when Williams had blasted another winner by her, Schiavoni turned to the ball boy, who offered her tennis balls for the next serve. Rather than take the balls, she beckoned him closer and said she needed a hug. That is often what we need amid the exasperations of life. The burden is too great. The gentle Servant offers just that.

Jesus does not lord it over us as a tyrant barking orders. He is with us in grace to guide us and help us in the demands of the Christian life. Often, we feel uneasy when our boss is looking over our shoulder. But our Lord doesn't just watch us—He watches over us. The yoke of discipleship is not onerous because Jesus is with us. He lifts the burden of oppressive legalism to make the obedience a delight.

Paul defends the legitimacy of his apostleship to the Corinthian church. In so doing, he doesn't assert his apostolic authority as he might. Rather, he appeals to his readers in this way: "I, Paul, myself am pleading with you by the meekness and gentleness of Christ" (2 Cor. 10:1).

One of the metaphors the Bible gives us for Jesus is a lion. He is the Lion of Judah. A lion does not comport well with our concept of gentleness. Yet that image gives us our firmest grasp for understanding the fruit.

Contrast two lions. One is the fearful feline of the classic story *The Wizard of Oz*. What sort of lion was he? He was a pussycat, all bluster and no bite. We meet him at his scariest. He jumps out at Dorothy and Toto and Scarecrow and the Tin Woodsman as they follow the yellow brick road to the Emerald City. He leaves them quaking in their boots with his fearsome roars and menacing presence. It is when he sets his sights on the little dog, Toto, that Dorothy stands up to him. She takes him to task for his bullying, and her chastisement leaves the lion whimpering. We learn he has no courage. His sudden gentleness is revealed as nothing but cowardice.

The other lion is the title character of C. S. Lewis's book *The Lion, the Witch and the Wardrobe*. His name is Aslan. In the book, the children who have entered Narnia through the wardrobe are conversing with Mr. Beaver. They ask him, "Who is Aslan?"

Mr. Beaver replies, "Well, Aslan is the King and the Lord of the whole wood, Narnia." He goes on to explain, "You see, Aslan is not just a lion, but he's a great Lion. He's the King of the beasts, and the real ruler of Narnia."

Susan asks, "Is he safe?"

Mrs. Beaver chimes in, "If there's anyone who can appear before Aslan without their knees knocking, they're either braver than most or else just silly."

Lucy repeats her sister's concern: "Then he isn't safe?"

"Safe," replied Mr. Beaver. "Who said anything about safe? Course he isn't safe. But he's good. He's the King, I tell you."

Aslan is gentle not because of cowardice but because of goodness and authority to serve. Jesus is better depicted not as the lion of Oz but the lion of Narnia. Gentleness does not mean toothless or tame. It means controlled strength and authority. Gentleness is governed by good.

In one of his Suffering Servant passages, Isaiah paints a remarkable portrait of Jesus in His gentleness. Remember, this is the same One who in Isaiah 9 will sit on the throne of David and be given an everlasting kingdom, the Son who is called "Wonderful, Counselor, Mighty God, Everlasting Father, Prince of Peace" (Isa. 9:6–7). Of this mighty One we read in Isaiah 42:1–3:

> Behold! My Servant whom I uphold,
> My Elect One in whom My soul delights!
> I have put My Spirit upon Him;
> He will bring forth justice to the Gentiles.
> He will not cry out, nor raise His voice,
> Nor cause His voice to be heard in the street.
> A bruised reed He will not break,
> And smoking flax He will not quench;
> He will bring forth justice for truth.

Reflect on this image a moment. What is a bruised reed like? It hangs limp, by a thread. Any rough handling will cause it to break off. Or, what is a faintly burning wick like, as some understand "smoking flax"? Think of when you first try to light a candle. The fledgling flame tries to take hold. The fragile spark flickers. You might even cup your hands around it, lest the slightest breeze extinguish it.

That's the gentleness of Jesus. He does not treat us as our sins deserve. Though we are laid down with guilt and shame, He receives us in the soil of our sin. He reasons with us that though our sin is as scarlet, it will be as white as snow. He cleanses us from all sin. He clothes us in the garments of His spotless righteousness. Though the flame of our faith flickers to failing, Jesus helps us in our unbelief. Though we are weak, He is strong for us. Though we are foolish, He is wise with us.

As we noted at the outset, sometimes the word translated "gentleness" is rendered "meekness." What image springs to mind when you hear the word *meek*? We might think of timid or docile, someone who is the wallflower of the party. We associate meek with weak. Such meekness is nonassertive and ineffectual.

The fruit of meekness/gentleness is anything but. As we look at Jesus, we see gentle strength. It is power and authority restrained with love and grace. Gentleness does not use its strength or authority to crush, but to handle with care.

Gentleness reflects how Jesus treats us. He came not to judge us—for who could stand? He came to be judged. He continues to treat us in our weakness and waywardness not with an iron fist, but with the firm grip of love. He does not manhandle us in our fears or sins or doubts or failures. He strives with us. He opens His arms to comfort us and uphold us. He is not safe. He is a warrior lion against His enemies. But He is a gentle Savior with those He loves.

How can we exhibit the gentleness of Jesus? What ripples of repercussions are created by our exercise of this fruit as it is cultivated through abiding in the Vine?

The Power of Gentleness

Peter does not use the word *gentleness* in the following verses, but he certainly gives us a good example of it in the model of Christ.

> The elders who are among you I exhort, I who am a fellow elder and a witness of the sufferings of Christ, and also a partaker of the glory that will be revealed: Shepherd the flock of God which is among you, serving as overseers, not by compulsion but willingly, not for dishonest gain but eagerly; nor as being lords over those entrusted to you, but being examples to the flock. (1 Peter 5:1–3)

Gentleness is not abusive. Rather, it exhibits sensitivity to others. It is compassionate and considerate, replete with mercy and grace.

The fruit of gentleness can draw others out. It creates an environment of embrace and openness. It invites vulnerability in others. It allows them to be real. Imagine sharing your deepest fears with someone, and he laughs at you or scorns you. You would not make that mistake again. But what if your fears were received with understanding, compassion, and concern? You would be blessed and your relationship with that person strengthened.

Let's explore some of the soft hues of gentleness given in Scripture as it is applied to various situations.

How We Lead

In the model of Jesus, gentleness is a prominent characteristic of those who lead in His name. The apostle Paul lays out the qualifications for those who govern and shepherd Christ's church. Among them we find, "not violent,…gentle, not quarrelsome" (1 Tim. 3:3).

Abusiveness has no place among those who are to care for the sheep entrusted to them. Elders are to be understanding, knowing that they too are sinners saved by grace. They too are prone to wander, prone to leave the God they love. That's why Paul tells the Ephesian elders to watch first over *themselves* and then over those in their charge (Acts 20:28).

The leadership of Christ is servant leadership, laced with gentleness. Leaders must emulate the One who is gentle and lowly in heart. As Jesus shares the yoke of discipleship with them, so leaders must walk with the sheep as understanding helpers. Those with knees buckling under burdens (of their own making and those imposed upon them) should be cared for as bruised reeds or barely burning wicks.

Paul describes this approach to care: "Brethren, if a man is overtaken in any trespass, you who are spiritual restore such a one in a spirit of gentleness, considering yourself lest you also be tempted. Bear one another's burdens, and so fulfill the law of Christ" (Gal. 6:1–2). To be overtaken is to be caught. By *caught* the apostle does not mean discovered or apprehended. He means ensnared, like a bear caught in a trap from which it cannot extricate itself.

A gentle approach would not be condescending or accusatory. It would come seeing itself cut from the same cloth. Like a surgeon who takes care to set a broken limb, painful firmness may be needed, but the infliction of unnecessary pain would be avoided. So the skillful physician of the soul ministers by speaking the truth in love and attending in gentle perseverance.

How We Treat Others

It is disturbing to hear the vitriolic invective leveled against governmental leaders in public discourse. Scathing verbal muggings and personal character assassinations are commonplace, accepted, and even expected. Issues on which people differ soon reach the level of personal assault.

This acrimony is not limited to the secular realm. Rancor finds itself on the lips of Christians who join in the rhetoric. Such mean-spiritedness infects the discourse of the church itself when its members engage in gossip and personal attack.

Life in the Vine promotes a different approach for us as children of God. In the passage we saw earlier, the apostle calls us "to be subject to rulers and authorities, to obey, to be ready for every good work, to speak evil of no one, to be peaceable, gentle, showing all humility to all men" (Titus 3:1–2). We are to be courteous, not contentious, and gentle, not abusive.

Gentleness is the mark of those who are keenly aware that it is but by the grace of God they go. As I write this, a story of the behavior of a young woman at a music award show is provoking much discussion in the blogosphere. This performer once epitomized wholesomeness but has given herself over to a raunchiness that is viewed as excessive, even among her peers. There are comments castigating her. Others simply express horror, and some outrage. Voices for righteousness have spoken up, taking her to task. But there are others who lament, aching for her and grieving over the direction of our culture. These voices are seasoned with gentleness in a tone of reasoned concern.

How We Use Our Words

Gentleness affects not only our attitude toward others but the expression of that attitude through our words. It's interesting to note that when God speaks to the topic of anger in His Word, He often includes an admonition about our speech in the vicinity. For example, in Ephesians 4 Paul tells us to "be angry, and do not sin" (v. 26). Three verses later he says, "Let no corrupt word proceed out of your mouth, but what is good for necessary edification, that it may impart grace to the hearers" (v. 29). Words are powerful weapons in the uncontrolled hands of anger. Our speech can be destructive or constructive.

Words can hurt or heal. Just listen to James on the subject. He calls the tongue "an unruly evil, full of deadly poison" (3:8). Arsenic is present in the human body as a trace element, evidently for healthy functioning. Yet large amounts of it can kill. The tongue that can help and heal is the same tongue that can maim and murder.

Proverbs 15:1 instructs us, "A soft answer turns away wrath, but a harsh word stirs up anger." "Soft" has in view gentleness and sensitivity. Gentle speech diffuses wrath. Harsh speech pours accelerant on it. The power is in our hands to do either. Gentleness wields the sword of the tongue with constructive concern and deliberate caution.

How We Evangelize and Promote Truth

Scripture identifies four ways we are to deliver truth. After telling Timothy that all Scripture is God-breathed and useful for teaching, reproof, correction, and training in righteousness, Paul goes on to say that it is to be applied with "longsuffering" and "teaching" (2 Tim. 4:2). Patience to tolerate and instruction to guide make for constructive interaction. We find the other two ways in 1 Peter, where we are told to give a defense of the faith with "meekness" and "fear" (3:15). We've explained *meekness* as "gentle strength." Fear has to do with respect.

Gentleness and respect mean that we do not just talk *at* people or talk *down to* people—we talk *with* them. We patiently listen to understand, not giving an answer before we hear (Prov. 18:13). When we do hear, we apply God's teaching so that it can be received.

One of the things I liked so much about the dentist I went to for so many years was his gentleness. I had been to dentists who jammed the needle into my gum and quickly depressed the plunger so that the novocaine would assault the tissue. My dentist took his time. The result was a much more comfortable mouth when the numbness wore off.

Knowing that the reception of truth and the effectiveness of the gospel don't depend on our pushiness should be an encouragement to gentleness. We must allow room for the grace of God and the conviction of the Spirit. When we dialogue with people on emotional issues, our conversation should be gentle, respectful, and seasoned with grace. We can strong-arm no one into the kingdom.

How We Conduct the Whole of Our Lives in Wisdom

James is a book on wisdom. The apostle begins by writing that we should consider it all joy when we encounter trials of various kinds, but he goes on to speak of the wisdom necessary by which we might do that. In fact, he differentiates between wisdom that comes from God, and wisdom that is demonic. The former is received by asking God for it in the application of His truth. The latter is pseudo-wisdom that will promote only an appearance of godliness and serve our own ends.

Here is James's recap of wisdom and its counterfeit: "This wisdom does not descend from above, but is earthly, sensual, demonic. For where envy and self-seeking exist, confusion and every evil thing will be there. But the wisdom that is from above is first pure, then peaceable, gentle, willing to yield, full of mercy and good fruits, without partiality and without hypocrisy. Now the fruit of righteousness is sown in peace by those who make peace" (3:15–18). Gentleness exhibits a wisdom that rests on God and pursues His ends.

Gentleness permeates the whole of Christian life as it is lived in the wisdom of God. We could say it is "laid back," rolling with God's providence and trusting in His strength. It lives in the courage of faith. It shows great strength in the face of provocation. It can be assertive without being abrasive.

Practicing Gentleness

Let's consider a case study of gentleness. A dad found out his teenage son possessed marijuana. The mom had been straightening the son's room and discovered a baggie of the stuff and some paraphernalia tucked away. Mom was worried, and Dad was angry. He was especially exercised because they had talked about this before, and the son had apparently been lying to his face.

How does the tandem of mercy and grace come into play to show gentleness? Several manifestations come to mind.

- Instead of cornering his son when he walked in the front door, a gentle father would push the pause button to get his anger under control. He might spend time in prayer asking God for the wisdom and grace needed to help in the time of need. He might talk it out with his wife to benefit from her counsel and to be on the same page.

- Instead of asserting his authority and lording it over his son, a gentle father would engage his son with respect and patience. He would listen before leaping. It may well be there is an explanation other than the obvious. Gentleness would also allow the father to hear the tone of fear, need, relief, or defiance in his son's voice.

- Instead of attacking his son with harsh or demeaning words, a gentle father would give thought to how Jesus has treated him in his own sin and failures.

- A gentle father's conversation would be full of grace, not to excuse what the son did but with an eye to help. His approach would be driven by love with a goal to restore.

Gentleness is like the foot on the accelerator that eases forward rather than barreling ahead to cause great destruction.

We find an example in the apostle Paul. Paul and his coworkers were ministering to the church at Thessalonica. As an apostle, Paul was in a position of authority. He had the right to make demands of them. He could take them to task. But Paul took another tact: "We were gentle among you, just as a nursing mother cherishes her own children" (1 Thess. 2:7).

Think about that image: a nursing mother taking care of her children. That is the gentleness of Christ we are called to emulate and cultivate in our dealings with others. That's the gentleness we need to confess our lack of and that we need to pray for greater measure of in ourselves and in our siblings in Christ.

Cultivating Growth

1. What is the gentleness that God wants us to display in our dealings with others?

2. How is gentleness exhibited in Jesus?

3. How does Isaiah 42:1–3 help us to understand and apply gentleness?

4. What contrast is made between the lions of Oz and Narnia?

5. What words would you use to describe the opposite of gentleness?

6. How does gentleness relate to leadership? To our treatment of others? To our speech? To our evangelism?

7. How does the case study of the father's dealing with his son showcase gentleness?

Chapter 11

Self-Control or Willpower?

For God has not given us a spirit of fear,
but of power and of love and of a sound mind.
Therefore do not be ashamed of the testimony of our Lord,
nor of me His prisoner,
but share with me in the sufferings for the gospel
according to the power of God,
who has saved us and called us with a holy calling,
not according to our works,
but according to His own purpose and grace
which was given to us in Christ Jesus before time began.

—2 TIMOTHY 1:7–9

What comes to your mind when you think of self-control? I tend to think of that last piece of cake on the platter. I know I shouldn't have it. I don't need the calories. Plus, it's almost bedtime, the worst time to be piling on calories. And it would be my third piece. I need to exert self-control. Is that all self-control is, stubbornness of will? How does it fit in as a fruit of the Spirit, sanctifying us in Christlikeness? How is it different from sheer willpower?

Self-control is more than an internal police force. It manages the operation center of the believer's heart.

Not Just Willpower

Willpower is by definition "self-discipline." It looks to exertion of the will for restraint. The "Just Say No" campaign to address drug abuse was an appeal to willpower.

Willpower is a secular version of self-control. Self-control is a fruit of the Spirit for management of self in the strength of Christ. Willpower is seated in the natural man, while self-control is rooted in the Vine and is a product of abiding in it. It enables the believer to wage war against the deeds of the flesh.

In Romans 6, Paul expresses the power of sin that remains in our flesh and uses himself to illustrate that power in Romans 7. In his treatment of the fruit of the Spirit in Galatians, the apostle lays out the means given us by God to do battle with those self-serving desires that plague us while we are in this world: "I say then: Walk in the Spirit, and you shall not fulfill the lust of the flesh. For the flesh lusts against the Spirit, and the Spirit against the flesh; and these are contrary to one another, so that you do not do the things that you wish" (Gal. 5:16–17). Self-control operates in the power of the new life to combat the desires of the flesh that are oriented to us rather than Christ.

In a visit to the garden of Gethsemane, we can see the limitations of willpower that has its seat in the flesh. Jesus had arrived at the garden on His way to the cross. He withdrew with three of His disciples to this special place to gird

Himself for what lay ahead. He told Peter, James, and John to wait while He went deeper into the garden for private communion with the Father. While Jesus was pouring out His heart in prayer, anguishing in the moment, the three disciples were struggling to keep their eyes open. Jesus' assessment was, "The spirit indeed is willing, but the flesh is weak" (Matt. 26:41).

What that tells us is that no matter how long we resist, no matter how hard we try, our natural resolve is not the place to find the control our God wants of us. Right there in the garden, Jesus points us where to find the strength we need when He calls us to "watch and pray."

Evidently Paul's young protégé, Timothy, was on the timid side. As a pastor he would face some daunting challenges. Paul did not exhort him to "man up" and tough it out. He didn't summon Timothy to inner resources of toughness. Rather, he said this: "For God has not given us a spirit of fear, but of power and of love and of a sound mind" (2 Tim. 1:7). The word translated "sound mind" carries the sense of discipline or self-management and is sometimes rendered "self-control."

Paul directs Timothy outside of his own will, efforts, and ability to the Spirit who indwells him. The power, the love, and the self-control are not of Timothy. They are all of God.

Does the fact that our strength and resolve are found in God and not ourselves relieve us of personal responsibility or effort? Not at all. It embeds them in Christ. In his letter to the Philippians Paul says, "I can do all things through Christ who strengthens me" (4:13). In John 15:5 Jesus insists that apart from Him we can do nothing. We are the doers, but in complete and continual dependence on Christ. As we abide in the Vine we find our strength both to will and to do as we live out our salvation in sanctification.

The Driver's Seat of Discipleship

Texting while driving is a scary prospect. I saw one commercial where a driver looks up from a momentary check of a text she received only to see a pedestrian ten feet in front of her. A photo making its way around the Internet shows a sports car rammed up to its windshield under the back of a tractor trailer. The caption reads: "Please don't text and drive." Whether or not the accident really did result from texting, it makes the point.

That point can also relate to the place of self-control in our Christian discipleship. Self-control keeps its hands on the wheel and its eyes on the road. Jesus said that those who follow Him must deny themselves and take up their cross. The cross does not refer to some special burden we bear in life. It speaks to bringing all of life into submission and service to the Father's will, as did Jesus. The cross shows the extent of that submission.

As citizens of heaven, those in the world but not of it, we are to seek the kingdom of God in all we do. That speaks to our ethics, our values, our priorities, our ambitions, our actions, our words—even our thought life. The twists and dangers of the path before us require that we make constant choices in which we are called to deny self and follow Christ. Self-control relates not just to the denying of self but also to the following of Christ.

For example, we might not feel like carving out time for prayer. Only the constraint of a mind set on things above will exercise the sound judgment that will turn off the television for half an hour in order to pray. Assessing the extra piece of cake will not be only a matter of our waistline but will relate to gluttony as we factor in what our Lord desires of us. Paul contrasts serving Christ with serving our own appetites (Rom. 16:18).

As long as we are in the flesh—that is, in this fallen world—we will have a bent to waywardness. The body of sin that remains will assert itself to seek our way, our will, and our wants. It's like a car whose wheels are out of alignment. We must keep a firm grasp on the wheel lest it veer off into a ditch, causing harm and keeping us from progress on the road set before us.

Freedom, Not Bondage

Some equate self-control with shackles. Life is all about "thou shalt not." Self-control takes on the role of a chaperone keeping us from having fun. Actually, self-control has more to do with protecting the freedom we have in Christ. It's not about bondage, but emancipation.

If we could return to our cake example: Imagine that you just lost fifty pounds through the discipline of diet. Before, food, especially sweets, used to rule you. But you've adopted a new outlook with a new direction. Self-control is not just about the sweets or the pounds. It's about being true to your new approach to life. In this way, self-control protects you from what harms you and formerly ruled you. Positively, it keeps you healthy and enjoying your newfound freedom.

The context for the fruit of the Spirit in Galatians 5 couches things in terms of liberty and living in light of that freedom: "Stand fast therefore in the liberty by which Christ has made us free, and do not be entangled again with a yoke of bondage.... For you, brethren, have been called to liberty; only do not use liberty as an opportunity for the flesh, but through love serve one another" (Gal. 5:1, 13). Self-control is not a slave driver. It is a freedom fighter.

It is the means by which we do not allow sin to reign over us, but instead live out our new life in righteousness. Paul labors to make the point: "Therefore do not let sin reign in your mortal body, that you should obey it in its lusts. And do not present your members as instruments of unrighteousness to sin, but present yourselves to God as being alive from the dead, and your members as instruments of righteousness to God. For sin shall not have dominion over you, for you are not under law but under grace" (Rom. 6:12–14). Self-control is not under law. It is under grace, having been set free from sin to serve our God in righteousness. It heeds the direction of our Father in heaven, who disciplines us as His children to conform us to the image of Christ.

Self-control is more than restraint. It is retraining for a life emancipated from the bondage of sin and participating in new life in Christ. In union with the Vine, this fruit mandates that we don't grow as a wild shoot in whatever direction we please, but that we grow in accordance with the Vine.

Wisdom literature gives us a helpful image to appreciate the rule of self-control. Proverbs 25:28 says, "Whoever has no rule over his own spirit is like a city broken down, without walls." Cities without walls in the ancient world were easy prey. Walls had to do not with bondage but with safeguarding. The wall kept the enemy out and allowed for peace and prosperity within its boundaries. It protected against those who would take away the citizens' freedoms.

Self-Control on Duty

Bruce is in his late forties. He has been married for seventeen years and has three kids. He is a believer. Raised in a Christian home, he can't remember a day when he did not know and trust in Jesus Christ as his Savior. He married his high-school sweetheart, also a believer. Both are very active in their local church and are respected and looked up to by everyone who knows them.

But Bruce has a secret life. He's covered his tracks, but if the firewall of his computer could talk, it would describe hundreds of pornographic sites that he has visited. Sometimes he will restrain himself for a few days, recently even for a couple of weeks. He feels pretty good about his efforts. But then the stress builds up and the desires of the flesh start demanding. Bruce gives in—again.

He knows he is doing wrong. He finds what he's doing repulsive. He even has a certain degree of self-loathing. He hates himself for it. He knows he is breaking covenant with the wife of his youth. He would be devastated if others knew. How would his wife react if she found out? What would his kids think of him? His reputation at church would be ruined. These thoughts spur Bruce on to try to get a handle on his vile habit.

Bruce has tried very hard and many times to stop. He has prayed and prayed that God would take this temptation from him. He's searched out Bible passages that speak to the subject. The one he's trying to memorize now is from Paul's first letter to the Thessalonians:

Finally then, brethren, we urge and exhort in the Lord
Jesus that you should abound more and more, just as
you received from us how you ought to walk and to
please God; for you know what commandments we
gave you through the Lord Jesus. For this is the will of
God, your sanctification: that you should abstain from
sexual immorality; that each of you should know how to
possess his own vessel in sanctification and honor, not in
passion of lust, like the Gentiles who do not know God;
that no one should take advantage of and defraud his
brother in this matter, because the Lord is the avenger
of all such, as we also forewarned you and testified. For
God did not call us to uncleanness, but in holiness.
Therefore he who rejects this does not reject man, but
God, who has also given us His Holy Spirit. (4:1–8)

He cringes to think that he is letting down his Lord and
grieving the Holy Spirit, by whom he was sealed for the day
of redemption.

Things have changed for Bruce in the last couple of
months. One, he realized he had to bring his struggles out
of the darkness, where they would thrive, into the light. He
shared his sin with others who loved him and would help him.
Two, Bruce took to heart what he had read in Romans 13:14
about making no provision to gratify the desires of the flesh.
He needed to use a computer, but he could go on it only when
others were around.

Third, Bruce came to realize that he was trying to resist
temptation in his own strength. He always thought he could
handle it. He admitted to himself that he could not. He
needed not just to resist. He needed to rest in the arms of the
One who loved him. Bruce began to fill his eyes with Christ.

He repented and returned to his first love. He saw his habit in terms of spiritual adultery. Bruce found solace and delight in the gospel that spoke to what Jesus did rather than what he did or could ever do.

Finally, Bruce's prayer life changed from nicety to necessity. It took on an urgency. He had to watch and pray. In his flesh he was weak. In his Savior he was strong. He discovered the psalms were full of prayers that captured his struggle—for example, Psalm 141:3–4:

> Set a guard, O LORD, over my mouth;
> Keep watch over the door of my lips.
> Do not incline my heart to any evil thing,
> To practice wicked works
> With men who work iniquity;
> And do not let me eat of their delicacies.

Bruce has come a long way. The inclination remains. He knows the danger of scratching that itch when it flares up. Even a little scratch will enflame it and prompt an ache for more. He knows that Jesus is his hope, his help, and, increasingly, his heart's desire.

Cultivating Growth

1. What is the difference between self-control and willpower?

2. As a soldier is marked by self-discipline, how does self-control help us in combating the flesh through the strength of the Holy Spirit (Gal. 5:16–17)?

3. What does Jesus tell us in the garden of Gethsemane about the pursuit of self-control?

4. Where do passages like John 15:5; Philippians 4:13; and 2 Timothy 1:7 lead us to find self-control?

5. How does the image of a car out of alignment impress upon us the importance of self-control?

6. Evaluate this statement: "Self-control is not a slave driver; it is a freedom fighter."

7. What has Bruce learned about the exercise of self-control in his struggle with pornography?

Chapter 12

Potent Humility

God resists the proud, but gives grace to the humble....
Humble yourselves in the sight of the Lord,
and He will lift you up.

—JAMES 4:6, 10

We now move from the garden planted in Galatians 5 identified as the "fruit of the Spirit." That does not mean, however, that we have exhausted the traits of Christian character God has for us. We might consider righteousness, holiness, knowledge, contentment, and godliness. As with all the fruit of life in Christ, each describes us by virtue of our union with Him, and each makes demands of us in our walk with Him.

As we step out of the garden of Galatians 5, however, we take stock of something that is itself a fruit of God's grace but also impregnates the whole. It promotes growth and function as it permeates each plant from which fruit is produced. That fruit is humility.

Humility acts as chlorophyll to a plant. Chlorophyll serves two primary purposes. One, it gives the plant its distinctive green color. Two, it enables the absorption of light and conversion of that light into energy, a process called photosynthesis.

As chlorophyll works in a plant to give it its distinctive color and allow it to grow and function in God's design, so humility gives believers their distinctive hue and helps them to thrive in the Vine. Every fruit of the Spirit is touched by humility. It is an essential element necessary for the production of the fruit of new life in Christ. Humility enables our abiding, drawing us to Christ, driving us to prayer, and drawing on the word of Christ to dwell in us richly. In that sense, it is not numbered among the listed fruit of Galatians 5, but it is present as a nutrient to all. In this chapter we explore the makeup of humility and how we can cultivate it in our lives.

The Orientation of Humility

If we were to put a plant on a table, we would discover that before long the flower would twist itself so that it angled toward the sun. A plant needs light and will seek it out.

Humility serves to orient us to the God of glory and Son of His love. It acts according to the word of the Lord that apart from Him we can do nothing. Only by abiding in the Vine will we live and grow and be able to operate according to His design.

Humility functions in the fear of the Lord. Such fear makes God large in our eyes. We are completely and continually dependent upon Him. We exist by Him and for Him. We live through Him. In Him we live and move and have our being.

The greater the presence of humility in our hearts, the greater we will see ourselves as debtors to grace and the more in awe of God we will be. James tells us that God "gives more grace," asserting that "God resists the proud, but gives grace to the humble" (4:6). Humility is a conduit of grace.

Jesus illustrates the posture of humility in His story of the Pharisee and the tax collector. The setting is the temple, and the scene is two men at prayer:

> "'The Pharisee stood and prayed thus with himself, 'God, I thank You that I am not like other men—extortioners, unjust, adulterers, or even as this tax collector. I fast twice a week; I give tithes of all that I possess.' And the tax collector, standing afar off, would not so much as raise his eyes to heaven, but beat his breast, saying, 'God, be merciful to me a sinner!' I tell you, this man went down to his house justified rather than the other; for everyone who exalts himself will be humbled, and he who humbles himself will be exalted." (Luke 18:11–14)

The Pharisee regarded himself highly. His tone was self-congratulatory. He was pleased with his actions, and he thought God should be as well. In contrast, the tax collector saw himself barren of anything to commend himself to God. He simply called to God for mercy. He had come to the realization Paul sets forth in his letter to the church at Corinth: "What do you have that you did not receive? Now if you did indeed receive it, why do you boast as if you had not received it?" (1 Cor. 4:7).

Humility operates in full recognition that it is a debtor to grace not only at the outset of the Christian life but in its ongoing. It necessarily exalts God and sees itself bankrupt in righteousness and devoid of merit. It operates in weakness that the strength of God might be obtained. We see this realization again in Paul's letter to the Corinthians: "And He said to me, 'My grace is sufficient for you, for My strength is made perfect in weakness.' Therefore most gladly I will rather boast in my infirmities, that the power of Christ may rest upon me. Therefore I take pleasure in infirmities, in reproaches, in needs, in persecutions, in distresses, for Christ's sake. For when I am weak, then I am strong" (2 Cor. 12:9–10). Paul's statement is humility driven. His deficiency and inadequacy put him in good position because they create dependence upon God and focus on Him.

Pride promotes foolish independence. Humility draws deeply upon the grace of God in communion with Him. James says that God opposes the proud—pride pits us against God. But humility opens us to Him for spiritual health and vitality in function. As the plant draws life from the large and brilliant sun, so we find ourselves warmed by God's presence. Isaiah 57:15 captures the scene:

> For thus says the High and Lofty One
> Who inhabits eternity, whose name is Holy:
> "I dwell in the high and holy place,
> With him who has a contrite and humble spirit,
> To revive the spirit of the humble,
> And to revive the heart of the contrite ones."

Humility establishes us in proper position to God, firmly rooted in the Vine. It looks to God for the production of the fruit of the Spirit. Indeed, with humility, that fruit will grow naturally and necessarily.

We might point out that this is a matter of frontline spiritual warfare for the believer. Our enemy the devil would stoke the flames of pride in our hearts, pitting us against God. That was his tactic in another garden, the garden of

Eden. James's counsel after saying that God opposes the proud but gives grace to the humble is this: "Resist the devil and he will flee from you. Draw near to God and He will draw near to you" (4:7–8). James calls us to lift our eyes to God as a plant does to the sun that we might draw upon His life-giving light.

Essential to the Body

There are certain things the body cannot do without. Contrary to popular opinion, morning caffeine is not one of them—but potassium is. Both human and plant cells need potassium to operate properly. It aids the cell in protein synthesis. It is remarkable to see all that this element does to contribute to a healthy functioning body in God's design.

In similar fashion, humility is essential to believers in their spiritual growth and in their function as disciples of Christ. Jesus said that to follow Him, a person must first take up his cross and deny himself. Humility inclines us to that. By it, we decrease and Christ increases (John 3:30). By it, we defer our will to our Lord's. Without humility we become hardened and resistant. We wither, we droop, and we experience listlessness and dryness.

The writer of Hebrews warns us of this hardening. "Beware, brethren, lest there be in any of you an evil heart of unbelief in departing from the living God; but exhort one another daily, while it is called 'Today,' lest any of you be hardened through the deceitfulness of sin" (Heb. 3:12–13). Humility prevents hardness of heart and wards off the deceitfulness of sin. By it we remain receptive, teachable, and malleable in the hand of our God to grow us in the image of Christ.

A serious health problem exists in the church today. God tells us that we are to love one another, rebuke one another, admonish one another, exhort one another, encourage one another, and confess our sins to one another. Christ's design for His body, the church, is mutual dependency.

But here's the problem. Have you ever tried to point out someone's sin to him? Perhaps you pulled a brother in Christ aside and said, "Jay, you treated your wife pretty harshly when we were out to dinner together the other night. Those words had to hurt her. What's going on?" If you said that in an effort to foster dialogue, how did that go for you? Was Jay receptive, eager to hear your observations? Our experience at such times is not openness in light of Hebrews 3, but defensiveness and rejection. Why? Because of a deficiency in humility. That deficiency cuts both ways. It can show up as a sense of superiority in the one admonishing and in resentment by the one being admonished. A lose–lose situation.

Humility promotes spiritual health and function not only in us as individuals but in the community of the saints. For all those "one another" passages we find in Scripture to be active and effective, humility must be in strong supply.

James's comments about humility are set in the context of conflict. He asks, "Where do wars and fights come from among you?" (4:1). Humility conspires with other fruit of the Spirit to disarm conflict and promote healing, as we see in Paul's urging: "Therefore, as the elect of God, holy and beloved, put on tender mercies, kindness, humility, meekness, longsuffering; bearing with one another, and forgiving one another, if anyone has a complaint against another; even as Christ forgave you, so you also must do. But above all these things put on love, which is the bond of perfection" (Col. 3:12–14). Our humility follows the pattern of our Lord in the power of the gospel. In Him, Paul shows us how to go about that.

Cultivating Humility

We've seen in our study of the fruit of the Spirit that each of the fruit comes to us as both a noun and a verb, a character trait and a command. We find both aspects in James 4. In verse 6 he speaks to "the humble." In verse 10 he bids us to humble ourselves. The humble are called to humility. The quintessential model is our Lord Jesus:

> Therefore if there is any consolation in Christ, if any comfort of love, if any fellowship of the Spirit, if any affection and mercy, fulfill my joy by being like-minded, having the same love, being of one accord, of one mind. Let nothing be done through selfish ambition or conceit, but in lowliness of mind let each esteem others better than himself. Let each of you look out not only for his own interests, but also for the interests of others. Let this mind be in you which was also in Christ Jesus, who, being in the form of God, did not consider it robbery to be equal with God, but made Himself of no reputation, taking the form of a bondservant, and coming in the likeness of men. And being found in appearance as a man, He humbled Himself and became obedient to the point of death, even the death of the cross. (Phil. 2:1–8)

As humbling Himself was the path to Christ's exaltation by the Father, so we follow that same path. In a passage that mirrors the one in James, Peter says, "Humble yourselves under

the mighty hand of God, that He may exalt you in due time"
(1 Peter 5:6). Exaltation is not gained by self-appointment, but
by the hand of God at His design. It is the pattern of the cross,
which is the wisdom and power of God to those who are being
saved (see Phil. 2:9; Heb. 12:2).

So how do we humble ourselves? James lays out three
ways to lead us in doing so by the power of the Holy Spirit.

Submission of Self

James instructs us first to submit ourselves to God. The word
for "submit" means "to subordinate oneself to" or "to yield to."
In submitting ourselves, we adopt a posture of servanthood.
Jesus is our ultimate example in this submission. Paul tells us
in Philippians that He "made Himself of no reputation, taking the form of a bondservant." Jesus "humbled Himself and
became obedient to the point of death, even the death on the
cross" (Phil. 2:7–8).

As we saw above, humility functions in the fear of the
Lord. Submission is the outworking of that fear. It recognizes
God for who He is and us for who we are—and acts accordingly. Jesus adopted this attitude of the fear of the Lord in His
incarnation. Isaiah, who prophesies the Messiah's virgin birth
(7:14) and princely mission (9:6–7), describes His mind-set:

> There shall come forth a Rod from the stem of Jesse,
> And a Branch shall grow out of his roots.
> The Spirit of the LORD shall rest upon Him,
> The Spirit of wisdom and understanding,
> The Spirit of counsel and might,
> The Spirit of knowledge and of the fear of the LORD.
> His delight is in the fear of the LORD,

And He shall not judge by the sight of His eyes,
Nor decide by the hearing of His ears. (11:1–3)

Our call is to take on the mind of Christ in submitting ourselves to God. Along with our Lord we insist, "Not my will, but Your will be done." We defer. We yield. We willingly pursue the will of our Father in heaven.

Pride, on the other hand, resists God. We can see why James couples submission to God with resisting the devil. Our minds harken to the enemy's tactics in the garden of Eden. Satan's ploy was to make Adam and Eve the arbiters of good and evil. He begins by bringing the word of God up for debate. "Has God indeed said?" Having engaged the woman, Satan contradicts God: "You will not surely die." The serpent pushed the wedge further by impugning the character of God. He suggests that God does not have their best interest at heart and is actually depriving them: "For God knows that in the day you eat of it your eyes will be opened, and you will be like God" (Gen. 3:1–5).

Satan presents competing counsel, and he markets his own as the way from darkness to light. Their eyes would be opened, he promised. All the while he lures our first parents from their place as created beings to oppose the Creator. In resisting the devil we submit to God, a practice illustrated by our Lord in the wilderness temptation. His reply was not even His own words—it was Scripture.

Orienting Ourselves to God

James goes on to say that we are to "draw near to God" with the assurance that in so doing, He will draw near to us. Having shaken ourselves of Satan's attempted molesting embrace, we now lift our eyes and run to the arms of our God.

"Return to Me, and I will return to you" is an Old Testament expression of contrition and recommitment (see, e.g., Mal. 3:7). This reminds us that sin is not just law-breaking. It is turning our back on God Himself, the Lawgiver. James begins his treatment on humility by speaking of those who have turned from God: "Adulterers and adulteresses! Do you not know that friendship with the world is enmity with God? Whoever therefore wants to be a friend of the world makes himself an enemy of God" (4:4).

The seeds of spiritual adultery lurk in the soil of our hearts. We are prone to wander, prone to leave the God we love. We are unlike Jesus, in whom there was no sin, because our motives are mixed and our best intentions are flawed. Even when we do resist the devil, we give ear to his temptations in a way Jesus did not. What that means is we can never let down our guard (see 1 Cor. 10:12). The faith by which we walk must be a repentant faith, turning from sin's pull to follow God.

When the writer of Hebrews wrote about God's discipline of us as His adopted children, he described what we are up against in our pilgrimage through this world.

> Therefore we also, since we are surrounded by so great a cloud of witnesses, let us lay aside every weight, and the sin which so easily ensnares us, and let us run with endurance the race that is set before us, looking unto Jesus, the author and finisher of our faith, who for the joy that was set before Him endured the cross, despising the shame, and has sat down at the right hand of

the throne of God. For consider Him who endured
such hostility from sinners against Himself, lest you
become weary and discouraged in your souls. (12:1–3)

Sin and obstacles weigh us down in our Christian walk. They
must regularly be accounted for and dealt with through confession and repentance. James puts it in stark terms that only
the humble will accept: "Draw near to God and He will draw
near to you. Cleanse your hands, you sinners; and purify your
hearts, you double-minded" (4:8).

Living in the Gospel

Like bread to a beggar, God promises grace to the humble. He
offers wisdom for the asking. Everything we need to face the
challenges of a God-honoring life is provided us by our God.
We are to fix our gaze on Christ, who supplies what is needed
to "increase the fruits of [our] righteousness" (2 Cor. 9:10) and
supplies "the Spirit" (Gal. 3:5), who grants us the resurrection
power of Christ (see Eph. 1:15–23).

All this is to say that we need to keep the gospel before us
as we keep in step with the Spirit in the cultivation of His fruit
in our lives. Notice the verbs James puts before us in verses 8
and 9 of chapter 4: "cleanse," "purify," "mourn," and "weep." He
is not only pointing out to us our sin and need for repentance,
but he is directing us to God for remedy for sin and provision
to press on. He is bidding us to live in the reality of the gospel. The blood of Christ cleanses us from all unrighteousness
(1 John 1:9). That cleansing is not found in mere confession of
sin, but in confession of Christ (1 John 2:1–2).

We can draw near to God only through the gospel of
Christ. He is our Mediator. The writer of Hebrews tells us

to look to Jesus for the race set before us. What does he have us see? We behold Jesus, who is the "founder and perfecter of our faith." He is seated as One who endured the cross in payment for our sin and is at the right hand of the Father in accomplished victory. He is the Jesus the writer of Hebrews has been describing for eleven chapters, who humbled Himself and delivered us from the power of reigning sin, who accomplished our salvation and gives us hope.

Our standing is in Christ, and our strength is in Christ. This is where humility takes us, stations us, and directs us to find our daily sustenance. As our bodies need to stay hydrated with water, our spirits need to stay hydrated with grace. The soil in which the fruit of the Spirit grows is saturated with the grace of the gospel, liberally applied through the irrigation of humility.

One last thought about this fruit of humility. One of the primary ways by which we abide in Christ for the bearing of fruit is prayer. Humility is requisite to prayer, as the writer of Chronicles highlights for us: "If My people who are called by My name will humble themselves, and pray and seek My face, and turn from their wicked ways, then I will hear from heaven, and will forgive their sin and heal their land" (2 Chron. 7:14).

Cultivating Growth

1. What is the fear of the Lord, and how does it relate to humility?

2. How is humility a conduit of grace?

3. What are some of the ways humility contrasts with pride?

4. What impact does humility have on the corporate level in the body of Christ?

5. What can we do to cultivate humility in our lives?

6. How does Jesus illustrate humility for us?

7. How do confession and repentance act to remove impediments to the flow of humility in our hearts, to our spiritual growth and vitality?

Chapter 13

Grace Grown

For the grace of God that brings salvation has appeared to all men,
teaching us that, denying ungodliness and worldly lusts,
we should live soberly, righteously, and godly in the present age,
looking for the blessed hope and glorious appearing of our great God
and Savior Jesus Christ, who gave Himself for us,
that He might redeem us from every lawless deed
and purify for Himself His own special people,
zealous for good works.

—TITUS 2:11–14

There is a movement in our society toward organically grown foods. Officially, *organically grown* refers to food grown and processed using no synthetic fertilizers or pesticides. Fruits and vegetables so grown are touted to be more nutritious, less harmful, and generally more healthful. *Organic* has become a technical term pointing to certifiably grown foods. It stands in contrast to those items called *natural*, which is not an officially recognized label and does not point to any standard. In some cases sellers use *natural* to counterfeit *organic*, hoping to appeal to the health conscious with this label.

When it comes to the growth of the fruit of the Spirit, we might employ the term *grace grown*. The fruit produced by grace is natural to new life rather than artificial. Such fruit grows organically at the hand of our Father, by the working of His Spirit, through union with Jesus Christ. To grow organically means to grow necessarily. The fruit of love, joy, peace, patience, and all the rest *will* grow as we abide in Christ, the product of God's workmanship of grace.

Not only will the fruit necessarily grow in the outworking of our salvation, it will be "much fruit, fruit that will last." A commercial for a certain plant food has a gardener standing between two tomato plants. One is green and healthy and laden with fruit. The other plant, however, looks like it's on steroids. It is lush and burgeoning with fruit. The difference, according to the ad, is the plant food. The narrator suggests this particular fertilizer will produce that sort of fruit for the entire growing season.

In consideration of the fruit of the Spirit, we have been examining the fruit. But we don't want to lose sight of the fact that it is the fruit *of the Spirit*. The risen and ascended Christ dwells in our hearts by the Spirit. That Spirit delivers us from bondage to sin and brings us into the redemptive kingdom of God. He unites us to Christ in our effectual calling. By Him we are adopted as sons and daughters of the living God. The Spirit empowers us with Christ's resurrection for the life God calls us to live. He gives spiritual gifts to His church for the welfare and work of the whole. And He grows us in Christlikeness through the grace of sanctification. We are told that the Spirit Himself is a seal and guarantee, the firstfruits of all that is ours in Christ (Rom. 8:23; Eph. 1:13–14).

Earlier in his letter to the Galatians, before taking up the fruit of the Spirit, Paul asks this rhetorical question: "Having begun in the Spirit, are you now being made perfect by the flesh?" (3:3). In Galatians 5:25 he says, "If we live in the Spirit, let us also walk in the Spirit." Paul is leading us to understand that our Christian maturation and fruitfulness do not happen at any point by self-effort to turn over a new leaf. Rather, we are dependent on the operation of the Holy Spirit.

To put it another way, we grow by grace. But what does that mean? We agree that sanctification is the work of God's grace by which we die more and more unto sin and live increasingly unto righteousness. But how does grace that rests fully on God, yet involves us, come into play? In the pastoral epistle addressed to Titus, Paul identifies the work of grace in our lives in two phases.

Grace-Enriched Soil

In Mark 4 Jesus relates the parable of the sower, which is more aptly named the parable of the soils. A farmer went out to sow seed. That scattered seed fell on four different surfaces. Some fell on the path and was quickly snatched up by birds. Some fell among rocky ground, but with little soil sprang up and quickly withered. Other seed fell among thorns. It showed life but yielded no fruit because the thorns choked it out. Yet other seed found its way to good soil. There it grew into hardy, fruit-producing plants.

Jesus explained the parable as the word of the gospel being sown. That which fell on the path was easy prey for Satan. That which fell among rocks and thorns gave the appearance of life, but did not thrive. Only the good soil yielded a harvest of fruit.

The soil is a metaphor for the human heart. How did the good soil become good? Clearly, by the operation of the Holy Spirit in the saving purpose of God (Mark 4:12; cf. John 12:40). The fruit that proceeds from a new heart is manifold. It brings glory to God.

In Titus 2:11, Paul speaks of the grace of God appearing. Certainly, that appearing refers to the incarnation of Christ: "And the Word became flesh and dwelt among us, and we beheld His glory, the glory as of the only begotten of the Father, full of grace and truth" (John 1:14). In Titus 3, Paul explains what appeared.

> For we ourselves were also once foolish, disobedient, deceived, serving various lusts and pleasures, living in malice and envy, hateful and hating one another. But when the kindness and the love of God our Savior toward man appeared, not by works of righteousness which we have done, but according to His mercy He saved us, through the washing of regeneration and renewing of the Holy Spirit, whom He poured out on us abundantly through Jesus Christ our Savior, that having been justified by His grace we should become heirs according to the hope of eternal life. (vv. 3–7)

As the grace of God appeared on the stage of human history, so that grace appears in our personal history by the regeneration and renewal of the Holy Spirit.

Those of us who came to Christ as adults can attest to the life-giving operation of the Holy Spirit. I was "churched" growing up. I heard the Bible stories and was catechized in doctrine.

I knew about Jesus and His birth, death, and resurrection. But after I was out of the house, I lost interest and stopped doing the "religious thing." I even became antagonistic to the faith and made it my business to argue with those who believed.

Then I met my wife-to-be, a committed Christian. I had never noticed one of those before. And she lived in a house with others like her. Through her and through the influence of others involved in Inter-Varsity Christian Fellowship at college, I saw a faith that flowed from the inside out. They were living epistles to me. I was exposed to biblical teaching.

I vividly recall one day in late October as I walked the grounds on my way back to my dorm. The truths of the gospel flooded my mind and spilled over to my heart. Rather than running off as they had before, the refreshing rains of God's grace soaked into my heart. The teaching of the Bible that had been so distasteful became delightful and desirable. I went back to my room, fell to my knees, and embraced the Christ that I was meeting for the first time.

What happened? What made the old, old truths come alive for me? They hadn't changed. There wasn't new news. I had changed, and not by my own effort. The Spirit of God had brought me from the state of spiritual deadness to spiritual life. He made me alive in Christ. He united me to the Vine, giving me ears to hear, a mind to grasp, a heart to embrace, and a will to receive Jesus Christ freely offered in the gospel. The apostle put it in stark terms in his letter to the church at Ephesus: "But God, who is rich in mercy, because of His great love with which He loved us, even when we were dead in trespasses, made us alive together with Christ (by grace you have been saved)" (Eph. 2:4–5).

Charles Wesley captures the divine intrusion of grace into our lives in his powerful hymn "And Can It Be."

> Long my imprisoned spirit lay
> Fast bound in sin and nature's night;
> Thine eye diffused a quick'ning ray,
> I woke, the dungeon flamed with light;
> My chains fell off, my heart was free;
> I rose, went forth and followed Thee.
> Amazing love! How can it be
> That thou, my God, shouldst die for me!

The grace that flowed from God brought to us the standing of justification, which pays for our sin and provides us with a perfect righteousness. It makes us children of God, heirs of life. Wesley captures this blessing in the next stanza.

> No condemnation now I dread;
> Jesus, and all in Him, is mine!
> Alive in Him, my living Head,
> And clothed in righteousness divine,
> Bold I approach th'eternal throne,
> And claim the crown, through Christ my own.

Grace comes to transform our hearts, unite us to the Vine, and enliven our spiritual senses. That grace arises exclusively and wholly from God—Father, Son, and Holy Spirit (Eph. 1:3–14). By grace He planted us in grace-enriched soil—good soil, soil that will bear fruit.

Grace-Enabled Growth

Having been grafted into the Vine is but the introduction to grace. The saving grace of Ephesians 2:8–9 leads to the sanctifying grace of Ephesians 2:10. They are a unit of God's salvation.

Paul explains how grace acts to grow us in Christ in Titus
2:11–14:

> For the grace of God that brings salvation has appeared
> to all men, teaching us that, denying ungodliness and
> worldly lusts, we should live soberly, righteously, and
> godly in the present age, looking for the blessed hope
> and glorious appearing of our great God and Savior
> Jesus Christ, who gave Himself for us, that He might
> redeem us from every lawless deed and purify for Him-
> self His own special people, zealous for good works.

Grace works in us from three vantage points.

Present Grace

Grace is said to have a training function in our lives. Some
translations express it as "training" rather than "teaching." The
Greek word is the same that we find in Ephesians 6:4, where
Paul tells fathers to bring their children up in the discipline,
or nurture, of the Lord. God is at work tending us as our
Father to cultivate in us a Christlike character.

What is the lesson plan of grace as a teacher? It is to
live in a manner worthy of our calling in Christ. We are to
renounce all that characterized us when we were dead in sin
(see Eph. 2:1–3; Titus 3:3), when we were in bondage to it and
in rebellion against God. Paul introduces the aspect of peda-
gogy when he gets down to practical matters in Ephesians.

> This I say, therefore, and testify in the Lord, that you
> should no longer walk as the rest of the Gentiles walk,
> in the futility of their mind, having their understand-
> ing darkened, being alienated from the life of God,
> because of the ignorance that is in them, because of the

blindness of their heart; who, being past feeling, have given themselves over to lewdness, to work all uncleanness with greediness.

But you have not so learned Christ. (4:17–20, emphasis added)

The traits Paul cites in Titus 2:12 are representative and symptomatic of the before and the after of our being in a state of grace. "Ungodliness and worldly lusts" speak to the traits of our life before Christ. "Soberly, righteously, and godly" refer to our new life in Christ.

What sort of teacher is grace? Grace does not lead us in some self-help course. On the contrary, grace leads us in Christ-dependence. It teaches us to abide in the Vine. Apart from Christ we can do nothing of our own accord. In Christ we can do all things according to His power that is at work within us. We work out our salvation with fear and trembling because God is at work in us.

Future Grace

We live now in light of the life to come. We wait for the blessed hope. Grace has laid up for us riches in glory. As we saw in 1 Peter, we have an inheritance kept for us, and we are kept for our inheritance. That is all of grace, a gift of God's giving.

The hope of eternal life is tethered to the grace of God, hammered into the ground of His saving purpose. Paul's letters to the Thessalonians lean toward future glory. Notice the role of grace in the finished product of God's sanctifying work:

Therefore we also pray always for you that our God would count you worthy of this calling, and fulfill all the good pleasure of His goodness and the work of faith with power, that the name of our Lord Jesus Christ may be glorified in you, and you in Him, according to the grace of our God and the Lord Jesus Christ....

Now may our Lord Jesus Christ Himself, and our God and Father, who has loved us and given us everlasting consolation and good hope by grace, comfort your hearts and establish you in every good word and work. (2 Thess. 1:11–12; 2:16–17)

Paul emphasizes: "According to the grace." "By grace." Grace that flows from the throne of a sovereign God floods our lives in Christ, bringing life where there was emptiness, lushness where there was barrenness, blessing where there was bleakness. Such grace empties into the basin of eternal glory.

By grace God holds us in His hand, and nothing can wrest us from it. By grace, God holds our hand between here and glory. He keeps us safe against the dangers of this present age, the efforts of the evil one to retake us, and the misalignment of sin that remains in our hearts. The grace that caught us up is the grace that attends our way and is the grace that will lead us home.

Past Grace

After showing us the work of God's present grace and the certainty of future grace, Paul urges Titus to keep before those he pastors past grace. This grace is bound up in the accomplished mission of Jesus Christ.

Paul identifies in Titus 2:14 a twofold cause of Christ's mission. First, He came to "redeem us from every lawless deed." He came to make rebels adopted sons and daughters. He broke the power of reigning sin in our lives. He led us as captives in His train, turning us from serving idols to know and serve the true and living God. He bought us at the price of His blood.

Second, Paul says Jesus came to "purify for Himself His own special people, zealous for good works." Grace so works in our lives to grant us new identities and new motivations. By the Spirit, the law of God is removed as a burden weighing us down and now stands written on our hearts. We become zealots for God, in service to His kingdom. There would be no good soil without the first appearance of Jesus and without the success of His redemption.

Grace, the Vine, and Abiding

When my older son, Luke, was in his first year at Geneva College in western Pennsylvania, he was assigned a dormitory roommate. They did not know each other before college. The contrast between the two was glaring. Luke was diligent in his studies, but his roommate rarely attended his classes. His academic effort was token, and his grades reflected that effort. He did not return for his sophomore year.

For both young men, the lessons were being faithfully taught by the Geneva professors. The difference between Luke and his roommate was that Luke showed up, ready, willing, and expectant of being taught. His roommate did not.

If grace is our teacher, it is incumbent upon us that we be good students. That involves not merely learning Bible stories. One of the tricks of academia that led me to succeed in my studies was studying not just the material but studying the tendencies of the professors as well. I learned their teaching style and emphases. I did things their way so that I would give them what they wanted.

In the same way, growing in Christ is not merely a matter of accumulation of knowledge about Him. It means growing to know Him. As Peter closes his second epistle, "Grow in the grace and knowledge of our Lord and Savior Jesus Christ. To Him be the glory both now and forever. Amen" (3:18).

We need to learn to abide—to rest in, remain, and regard our Lord in all things, at all times. We want to sit at His feet to learn both what He says and the heart by which He says it. We want to grow in submission to Him, dependence upon Him, and delight in Him.

Here's the problem—and it's a big one. A major way we abide is through prayer. Prayer is a means of grace. It is digestive juices to the reading of God's Word to our spiritual nourishment and growth in grace. Prayer helps us to be attentive to the voice of God. Through it we wrestle with understanding God's Word and the application of it. By prayer, we commune with our Lord.

To the degree we are negligent in prayer, we are derelict as students of grace. Either we don't show up, or we show up unprepared and unreceptive. Without prayer, we see ourselves in the mirror of God's Word, but we quickly forget what He has shown us of ourselves in it. If prayer is not a tool of our learning, the doctrine we learn becomes cold, dry, insipid, and irrelevant. We have left our first love. We may be attached to the Vine, but we are not abiding in it for the fruitfulness our Father desires.

Prayer reminds us that abiding is not merely connecting to a source of power, like a plug to an outlet. Abiding is more than drawing upon resources outside of ourselves. To abide is to commune with our personal, living Lord. Without ceasing, we seek His care and wisdom and strength in the trenches of life. We engage Him in sweet fellowship, expressing to Him our fears and failures and frustrations. We cry out to Him and hear the assurances of His presence and peace and provision, as He reminds us that He is the Vine in whom we have been grafted by grace.

The Psalms give voice to our abiding, informing our perspectives and directing our steps as they touch on the breadth of life in interaction with Him whose we are.

> Blessed is the man whose strength is in You,
> Whose heart is set on pilgrimage.
> As they pass through the Valley of Baca,
> They make it a spring;
> The rain also covers it with pools.
> They go from strength to strength;
> Each one appears before God in Zion.
> O LORD God of hosts, hear my prayer;
> Give ear, O God of Jacob!
> O God, behold our shield,
> And look upon the face of Your anointed. (Ps. 84:5–9)

Without prayer, an effort to renounce ungodliness and worldly passion and instead live self-controlled, upright, and godly lives in the present age will be in our own strength, on our own terms, for our own ends. The result will be fruit that is underdeveloped, malnourished, and even nonexistent. On a corporate level, the local church will be lethargic and ineffective.

We close our consideration of the fruit of sanctification with Paul's prayer toward its growth in fruitfulness through abiding in the Vine:

> And this I pray, that your love may abound still more and more in knowledge and all discernment, that you may approve the things that are excellent, that you may be sincere and without offense till the day of Christ, being filled with the fruits of righteousness which are by Jesus Christ, to the glory and praise of God. (Phil. 1:9–11)

May that be our prayer for ourselves, our brethren, and our spiritual leaders as we purpose to abide in the Vine that we might bear fruit—much fruit, fruit that will endure, to the glory of our God.

Cultivating Growth

1. To what does the label *grace grown* point?

2. What does it mean for the fruit of Christlike character to be the fruit "of the Spirit"?

3. What does Jesus' parable of the soils tell us about the soil that produces fruit? What caution does it hold?

4. How does Titus 3:3–7 convey what God has done in the soil of our hearts by His mercy and grace?

5. How does grace relate to our engrafting into the Vine and abiding in the Vine?

6. What three aspects of grace does Paul present in Titus 2:11–14, and what value does each hold for our spiritual growth?

7. What place does prayer hold for our abiding in the Vine?

Stanley D. Gale is the husband of one wife (Linda), father of four children (Samantha, Luke, Sarah, Nathan), and grandfather of eight (Ruby, Isaac, Weston, Kaylie, Jasper, Asher, Gryphon, Penelope). He holds bachelor of arts and master of education degrees from the University of Delaware, a master of divinity degree from Westminster Theological Seminary in Philadelphia, and a doctor of ministry degree from Covenant Theological Seminary in St. Louis. He is an ordained pastor in the Presbyterian Church in America and has served his current charge in West Chester, Pennsylvania, since 1988. He has authored books on prayer, spiritual warfare, evangelism, and the biblical worldview (Ecclesiastes), in addition to a variety of articles. He blogs semi-regularly on his Community Houses of Prayer website (http://www.CHOPministry.net) and can be contacted at SDGale@CHOPministry.net.